Wonders and Miracles

A Passover Companion

ILLUSTRATED
WITH ART SPANNING
THREE THOUSAND YEARS

WRITTEN AND COMPILED BY

Eric A. Kimmel

SCHOLASTIC PRESS ♦ NEW YORK

Permission to use the following materials has been granted by the copyright holders: J. Patrick Lewis for "Spirit of the Seder." Copyright © 2000 by J. Patrick Lewis. ♦ Robert Rubinstein for "The Passover Guest." Copyright © 1994 by Robert Rubinstein. Nina Jaffe for "The Hebrew Midwives." Copyright © 1999 by Nina Jaffe. ♦ Gershon Levine for "And You Shall Teach Your Children." Copyright © 1998 by G.A. Levine. ♦ Malka Schaps for "Alone in the Castle." Copyright © 1998 by Mary Schaps. David Schaps for "Grandma Tirzah Remembers." Copyright © 1998 by David M. Schaps. ♦ Linda Kaufman and Carla Silen for "A Million Questions (More or Less)." Music copyright © 1998 by Linda Kaufman. Lyrics copyright © 1998 by Carla Silen. Peninnah Schram for "Elijah The Builder" from *Jewish Stories One Generation Tells Another.* Copyright © 1987, 1993, 1996 by Peninnah Schram. ♦ Sadie Rose Weilerstein for "A Passover Mix-up" from *The Best of K'tonton.* Copyright © 1980 by Sadie Rose Weilerstein. ♦ Sounds Write Productions, Inc. (ASCAP) for the following music and lyrics by Debbie Friedman: "Miriam's Song" and "Kadish D'rabanan" from *And You Shall Be a Blessing,* copyright © 1988 Deborah Lynn Friedman; "I Am the Afikoman" from *Shanah Tovah: A Good Year,* copyright © 1987 Deborah Lynn Friedman; "The Promise" from *The World of Your Dreams,* copyright © 1991 Deborah Lynn Friedman. All ASCAP. "Kadish D'rabanan" and "Miriam's Song" also found on *The Journey Continues,* a Passover recording with other original and traditional songs for the holiday (www.debbiefriedman.com).

LIBRARY OF CONGRESS CATALOGING-IN-PUBLICATION DATA

Wonders and miracles: a Passover companion / compiled by Eric A. Kimmel.— 1st ed. p. cm. Summary: Presents the steps performed in a traditional Passover Seder, plus stories, songs, poetry, prayers, and archival pictures that celebrate the historical significance of this holiday to Jews all over the world. Includes bibliographical references and index. ISBN 0-439-07175-5 1. Passover—Juvenile literature. 2. Seder—Juvenile literature. 3. Judaism—Juvenile literature. 4. Haggadah. [1. Passover. 2. Seder. 3. Holidays. 4. Judaism—Customs and practices.] I. Kimmel, Eric A. BM695.P3 W66 2004   296.4'37—dc21   2002004732

10 9 8 7 6 5 4 3 2   04 05 06 07 08

Printed in Singapore   46 ♦ First edition, February 2004 ♦ The text type was set in Adobe Garamond. The interior display type was set in Francesca. The jacket display type was hand lettered by Don Marsh. The Hebrew type was set by Warren Wolfsohn at Nostradamus Advertising. Book design by David Caplan

ACKNOWLEDGMENTS: Special thanks to my editor, Dianne Hess, and to Steve Diamond, Sarah Longacre, and Jessica Moon from Scholastic's photo research department for all their hard work and stamina in tracking down the art; Professor Stefanie Siegmund of The University of Michigan for her historical consultation on the art; Rabbi Benay Lappe for her meticulous fact-checking of the manuscript; Havva Charm and Sharon Mintz from The Library of the Jewish Theological Seminary; Debbie Friedman, Sharon Friedman, Rabbi Nancy Wiener, Sharon Pollack, William W. Hess, and Shirley E. Hess for their generous help with the project; and David Caplan, for his stunning book design.

ABOUT THE FRONT JACKET: Moses with the Ten Commandments and his brother Aaron. Aaron, who is associated with the priesthood, is often depicted with sacred objects. This illustration is a twenty-first century adaptation of a 1734 German Haggadah, which echoes the design of the frontispiece of the Sulzbach Hagaddah of 1711, which then imitated the Amsterdam Haggadah of 1695. Ironically, the pictures from the Amsterdam Haggadah (which were copied and imitated more than any Haggadah in history) were illustrated by a Jewish convert who copied his illustrations from a Christian source.

♦ ♦ ♦

FOR DORIS,
WHO MAKES
THE BEST
SEDER

TABLE OF

CONTENTS

⊰ CONTINUED ⊱

It shall be that when you come to the land that God has promised, you shall observe this service. . . .

— Exodus 12:25

נזכרים

היינו

לפרעה במצרים ויוציאנו

יי אלהינו משם ביד חזקה

ובזרוע נטויה ולא הוציא

INTRODUCTION

Passover, many would say, is the most important holiday of the Jewish year. It marks the moment when Israel became a nation, when the descendants of Abraham, Isaac, and Jacob emerged from slavery in Egypt to change the course of history.

Passover is a holiday of liberation, like America's Fourth of July, Mexico's Cinco de Mayo, and France's Bastille Day. Families and friends come together to celebrate. The festival lasts seven or eight days. Preparing for it can take weeks.

Yet Passover differs from other national holidays. There are no picnics, fireworks, or marching bands. Passover is celebrated at home, at dusk, when streets empty and curtains are drawn across windows. It is a holiday filled with contradictions. It is a solemn religious event, but also a joyous feast. We celebrate our freedom from oppression, yet we do not rejoice over the sufferings of our oppressors.

All the members of the family, from the oldest to the youngest, take part in the Seder, the ritual Passover meal. Children play an important part, since the Torah requires us to tell them the Passover story.

The story is told in bits and pieces. Some of the most important parts are left out. Moses, the hero of the Exodus, is never mentioned during the Seder. His name does not appear even once in the traditional Haggadah (the collection of readings from the Bible and other writings) that is recited at this time.

Consequently, it is not surprising that many people attending a Seder for the first time — and even some who have celebrated Passover in their homes for years — miss the meaning of the many layers of ritual, tradition, and history underlying the Passover observance.

Passover is a holiday both ancient and modern; simple, yet rich in meaning and symbolism; timeless, yet ever-changing. Its traditions draw on centuries of history, art, and literature. The texts and illustrations used in this book come from all over the world and span 3,000 years.

This book was created to give people of all ages a fuller, richer understanding of what Passover means. The book should be read before the Seder, and used during the Seder together with the Haggadah, to answer questions that the participants might have. That is what the Seder is really about: asking questions, getting answers, expanding our knowledge and understanding.

And now, the day approaches its close. The streetlights are coming on. The house is cleansed of leaven. The table is set. It is time to gather round to remember our ancestors on a similar night long ago in ancient Egypt, when they started their journey from slavery to freedom.

The Seder begins.

"We Were Slaves unto Pharaoh in Egypt."
(Barcelona Haggadah. Northern Spain, mid-fourteenth century.)

אַחַת מִשֶּׁשׁ הַמַּצוֹת אֲ

אֲשֶׁר כָּסֵל וְכוֹצֵעַ אוֹתָהּ

לִשְׁתַּיִם וּמַנִּיחַ חֶצְיָהּ כֵּן

שְׁתַּיִם שְׁלֵמוֹת וְחֲצִי הַמַּ

הַמַּצָּה וְחוֹבֵס עָל שְׁנֵי

Spirit of the Seder

BY J. PATRICK LEWIS

Our house is cleansed, and we await

The celebration of the eight

Days of Pesach. Girl and boy

Anticipate the feast of joy.

Once again we praise the Giver,

Whose Gift of Gifts was to deliver

Us from ancient bondage, chains

That scarred the hard Egyptian plains.

Leave no family on its own

To celebrate the Feast alone:

Invite them all to see and hear it.

Share the freedom of the spirit.

As a family sits around the Seder table, the father breaks the middle matzah.
(Barcelona Haggadah. Northern Spain, mid-fourteenth century.)

Night Journey

Get ready. We are going on a journey. It will last only one night, but it will take us a long, long way.

We will travel from slavery to freedom.

From sorrow to joy.

From a country not our own to the land given by God to our ancestors.

For this is the night of Passover, the night when our ancestors left Egypt, the House of Slavery. They left on foot, in haste, carrying their belongings on their backs, driving their flocks and herds before them.

We are going with them. Our journey is called the *Seder*. Our guide is a special book called the *Haggadah*. It tells the Passover story.

Get ready. We are leaving soon.

Our journey is about to begin.

Here are two of the four colossal statues of Ramses II from the Great Temple of Abu Simbel in Egypt. Most scholars believe that Ramses II (1290-1224 B.C.E.) was the Exodus Pharaoh. Could this be the face of the ruler who spoke with Moses?

סימני סדר פסח

קדש

פר אין אונזין זאלטו קידוש א
אמכין :
דירה קידוש :

ורחץ

נית צו פר געטין דיא הענד צו
וועטין :
לאבדרה לקם מקוום קינו דירה ב
ברכה :

כרפס

איפוך טונק אין עסק אדר אמטיך
אונ׳ אנוך דיא ברכה בורא פרי
האדמה :
טומרה דיל אפיו קי אינטניירה קיכל
וינאגרי די דירה בורא פרי האדמה :

יחץ

די איטאלטי אלה פון אנדר טפלט
די העלפט צו אפיקומן אונטער די
זאן ביהאלט :
פרטירה לה מצה במורה די ק
ליכמידין קי מיטירה לה מידיה און
לוס מנטילים :

מגיד

דאז לויי אונ׳ זרוע פון בעקין ג
נעמן · אונ׳ זאג כהא איט הוכיר
טטים :
דירה לה הגדה :

רחצה

טן וועט די הענד · אונ׳ אנוך ג
נטילת ידים ביהענד :
די לאבדרה לקם מקוום קי דירה
על נטילת ידים :

מוציא מצה

אמך אוליו אובר די אובריטי אלה
אונ׳ נעם איין שטיק פון די הלב אלה
אונ׳ זאג לווילו ברכות :
דירה המוציא קיכלה דילינסימו קי ט
קומה פארטירה די לה מידיה די הל
מידיום קומרה טודוויינטו קי דירה על
אכילת מצה :

מרור

אטעיך אין חרוסת טונק איטכלין
איין ווייניג איז גנוגג :
קינטיירה די לה לינגוה קיכל ויאגרי
קי דירה על אכילת מרור :

כורך

נעם איין שטיק פון דר דריטי אלה
אונ׳ עט איט ביטר קרויט זאת ב
ביטטו יזלם :
טומרה די טודם קי די לה מצה קי ק
קינטיירה קיכל חרוסת קי דירה
זכר למקדש :

שלחן עורך

ריכט איין דיין טיש אונ׳ עט איט ע
ערין · ווערט דיר הש״י פֿון גוטט
בטערין :
קורדינארן לה מיזה :

צפון

נאך דז דו האטט גיגעסן זונדר :
זורגן עט איין שטיק פון אפיקומן
דער דאז איז פר בורגן :
קי קומרה קארה קונו קומטו קוט
קוייטונה :

ברך

אלט דוא האטט גיגעסן אפיקומן
זאלטט דו בענטשין איט א
אזומן :
דירה ברכת המזון :

הלל

די טיר זאלטט דו אויף אמכין
אונ׳ זאלטט זאגן שפוך פר אוי
זאכין :
דירה הלל :

נרצה

אונ׳ דיינו דיא הגדה פֿולענדן
בזכות זה ווערט אונט גאט א
משיח זענדן · אמפֿיר :
יהי לפני ה׳ לרצון :

Maps for the Journey

THE HAGGADAH

When travelers set out on a journey, they carry a map to show the way. The Haggadah is our map. The Hebrew word *haggadah* means "the telling." (*Haggodot* is plural.)

For our Seder to be complete and in "order" — which is what the word *seder* means — we must tell the entire Passover story, from beginning to end, leaving nothing out. We make sure to do this by following our map, the Haggadah.

The Haggadah opens with this simple rhyme. (Read the left column first, then read the right column.)

Kadesh ◆ קַדֵּשׁ	Maror ◆ מָרוֹר
Urchatz ◆ וּרְחַץ	Korech ◆ כּוֹרֵךְ
Karpas ◆ כַּרְפַּס	Shulchan Orech ◆ שֻׁלְחָן עוֹרֵךְ
Yachatz ◆ יַחַץ	Tzafun ◆ צָפוּן
Maggid ◆ מַגִּיד	Barech ◆ בָּרֵךְ
Rachtzah ◆ רָחְצָה	Hallel ◆ הַלֵּל
Motzi Matzah ◆ מוֹצִיא מַצָּה	Nirtzah ◆ נִרְצָה

The illustration on the left depicts the fourteen parts of the Seder. Versions of this picture have been found in Haggadot for hundreds of years. Look for sections of this picture throughout this book, as they signal the major parts of the service. Beginning with the top right, the sequence moves down the right side, then continues down the left side, and ends with the bottom picture, which reads from right to left. (Copenhagen Haggadah. Germany, 1739.)

The words of the rhyme are the parts of the Seder. The rhyme makes them easy to remember.

Now we know all the parts of the Seder by heart. What's the point? Why do we need to memorize them when we have the Haggadah?

People didn't always have a Haggadah. It is only within the last 600 years, with the use of the printing press and paper, that books have become cheap enough for most people to own. Before then, books were rare and expensive. Each one had to be written by hand on specially prepared animal skins called *parchment* and *vellum*. Only the wealthiest families could afford to have their own Haggadah.

Without a written guide to the Seder, how could people be certain they were doing everything in the correct order? How could they be sure they were not leaving anything out? The little rhyme "Kadesh Urchatz" solved this problem. The poem was easy to memorize and simple to write down. Even small children could learn it. Now everyone could have a map of the Seder. If a family followed the steps of this poem, their Seder would surely be complete.

This is what the fourteen parts of the Seder are about:

1. **Kadesh**: Making the festival holy. We light the candles and say several blessings, including the first of the four blessings over wine.
2. **Urchatz**: We wash our hands.
3. **Karpas**: We dip the greens, or parsley, in salt water and say the blessing. Then we eat it.
4. **Yachatz**: We break the middle matzah, setting aside the larger piece.
5. **Maggid**: We tell the Passover story.
6. **Rachtzah**: We wash our hands and say the blessing this time.
7. **Motzi Matzah**: We say the usual blessing for bread and a special blessing for matzah. We eat the matzah.
8. **Maror**: We dip the bitter herb in *charoset* (a fruit and nut mixture) and eat it.
9. **Korech**: We eat the bitter herb between two pieces of matzah.
10. **Shulchan Orech**: We enjoy the Passover meal.
11. **Tzafun**: We distribute the *afikoman*.
12. **Barech**: We say the blessings after the meal.
13. **Hallel**: We recite psalms of praise.
14. **Nirtzah**: We recite the closing prayer to end the Seder.

The Seder Plate

The Seder plate in the middle of the Passover table is another map for our journey. The objects on and around it help us to remember the Passover story.

1. **The Three Pieces of Matzah** represent the three ancient ranks of the Jewish nation. These are: (1) the *Kohanim,* the Priests, (2) their helpers, the Levites, and (3) the people of Israel.

2. **The Salt Water** reminds us of the sorrowful tears our ancestors shed when they were slaves in Egypt. It also reminds us of the miracle at the Red Sea.

3. **The Roasted Egg** stands for hope and new beginnings. It has been seared with fire. This teaches us that life is never easy. Great achievements come only after hard work and struggle.

4. **The Roasted Shank Bone** stands for the lamb that each Israelite family cooked and ate on the night of the first Passover.

5. **The Greens,** or parsley, are a sign of spring. On the night of the first Passover, Moses told the people of Israel to use bundles of leaves to smear the blood of the Passover lamb on the doorposts of their houses. The parsley reminds us of that night, when God "passed over" the homes of the Israelites to strike the Egyptians.

6. **The Horseradish's** bitter taste reminds us of how the Egyptians embittered the lives of our ancestors during the time of slavery.

7. *Charoset* is a sweet mixture of fruit, nuts, and wine. It reminds us of the mortar our ancestors used to bind together the bricks with which they built cities and temples for the Egyptians.

8. *Chazeret* is another type of bitter herb, usually lettuce. Because the Torah speaks of "bitter herbs," some families believe there should be at least two types of bitter herbs on the table. Freshly picked lettuce does not taste bitter. It acquires a bitter taste if it is allowed to go to seed. This symbolizes the experiences of our ancestors in Egypt. At first the Egyptians welcomed them. Only after many years did they make them into slaves. That is why we eat lettuce as well as horseradish, to remember the kindness of the Egyptian people, as well as the bitterness of slavery.

9. **Elijah's Cup** is the cup of wine in the center of the table. Elijah was a great prophet, whose coming will bring an age of peace. In some homes a cup of water is placed beside Elijah's Cup. This is called Miriam's Cup, in honor of Miriam, Moses' sister, who was also a great prophet.

This embroidered matzah cover depicts the Seder plate and the objects that appear on it. The banners at the top and bottom express holiday greetings. (India, nineteenth century.)

Aaron, high priest and brother of Moses, pours oil into a seven-branched menorah. As on the cover of this book, Aaron is usually depicted with sacred objects. (Illumination from the North French Miscellany. France, 1280.)

Kadesh

LIGHT THE CANDLES,
SAY THE BLESSINGS

The Seder begins. The holiday candles are lit. The blessing is recited:

בָּרוּךְ אַתָּה יְיָ אֱלֹהֵינוּ מֶלֶךְ הָעוֹלָם אֲשֶׁר
קִדְּשָׁנוּ בְּמִצְוֹתָיו וְצִוָּנוּ לְהַדְלִיק נֵר שֶׁל יוֹם טוֹב.

*Baruch ata Adonai, Eloheinu Melech ha-olam, asher kid'shanu b'mitzvotav
v'tzivanu l'hadlik ner shel yom tov.*

*Praised are You, God, Ruler of Creation, who has made us holy through
Your commandments, and commanded us to kindle the festival lights.*

We say a prayer thanking God for allowing us to celebrate this festival. Then we raise
our wine cups to recite the *Kiddush*, the blessing over the first of the four cups of wine
that we will drink during the Seder:

בָּרוּךְ אַתָּה יְיָ אֱלֹהֵינוּ מֶלֶךְ הָעוֹלָם בּוֹרֵא פְּרִי הַגָּפֶן.

Baruch ata Adonai, Eloheinu Melech ha-olam, borei p'ri ha-gafen.

Praised are You, God, Ruler of Creation, who creates the fruit of the vine.

בָּרוּךְ אַתָּה יְיָ אֱלֹהֵינוּ מֶלֶךְ הָעוֹלָם עַל הַגֶּפֶן
וְעַל פְּרִי הַגֶּפֶן וְעַל תְּנוּבַת הַשָּׂדֶה וְעַל אֶרֶץ
חֶמְדָּה טוֹבָה וּרְחָבָה שֶׁרָצִיתָ וְהִנְחַלְתָּ
לַאֲבוֹתֵינוּ לֶאֱכֹל מִפִּרְיָהּ וְלִשְׂבֹּעַ מִטּוּבָהּ
רַחֵם יְיָ אֱלֹהֵינוּ עַל יִשְׂרָאֵל עַמֶּךָ וְעַל
יְרוּשָׁלַיִם עִירֶךָ וְעַל צִיּוֹן מִשְׁכַּן כְּבוֹדֶךָ וְעַל
מִזְבְּחֶךָ וְעַל הֵיכָלֶךָ וּבְנֵה יְרוּשָׁלַיִם עִיר
הַקֹּדֶשׁ בִּמְהֵרָה בְיָמֵינוּ וְהַעֲלֵנוּ לְתוֹכָהּ
וְשַׂמְּחֵנוּ בְּבִנְיָנָהּ וְנֹאכַל מִפִּרְיָהּ וְנִשְׂבַּע מִטּוּבָהּ
וּנְבָרֶכְךָ עָלֶיהָ בִּקְדֻשָּׁה וּבְטָהֳרָה וּרְצֵה
וְהַחֲלִיצֵנוּ בְּיוֹם הַשַּׁבָּת הַזֶּה   וְשַׂמְּחֵנוּ בְּיוֹם
חַג הַמַּצּוֹת הַזֶּה כִּי אַתָּה יְיָ טוֹב וּמֵטִיב לַכֹּל
וְנוֹדֶה לְּךָ עַל הָאָרֶץ וְעַל פְּרִי הַגֶּפֶן
בָּרוּךְ אַתָּה יְיָ עַל הָאָרֶץ
וְעַל הַפֵּרוֹת

Four Cups

Why do we drink four cups of wine? Why not three or seven?

The traditional explanation is that we drink four cups of wine to celebrate God's promise of freedom. God told Moses to say to the Children of Israel, "I am God, and I will free you from the bondage of Egypt; I will deliver you from your servitude; I will redeem you with an outstretched arm and with great judgments. I will take you to be my people and I will be your God. And you will know that I am the Lord God who rescued you from the bondage of Egypt." (Exodus 6:6–7).

"I will free you . . . I will deliver you . . . I will redeem you . . . I will take you . . ." There are four parts to God's promise to free the Israelites from slavery. In honor of that promise, every Jewish person, no matter how poor, is required to drink four cups of wine at the Seder.

What if a person cannot drink wine? Can some other drink be substituted? That depends on the circumstances, as the following story shows.

This border of vines and grapes is from a lavish modern Haggadah that was created to resemble one from the Middle Ages. The man wears the conical "Jew hat," which Jewish men in many areas of medieval Germany were required to wear to distinguish them from the rest of the population. This hat appears in many of the pictures throughout the book. (Kafra Haggadah. New York, 1949.)

Milk for Wine

Brisk is the city of Brest Litovsk in Lithuania. This is one of the many stories told about Rabbi Hayyim Soloveichik (1853–1918). Rabbi Hayyim, also known as the Brisker Rav, was a towering figure of learning and spiritual leadership. He had time and a friendly word for everyone. No question was ever too simple; no one who needed help was ever turned away.

A poor man approached the rabbi of Brisk a few days before Passover. "Rabbi," he said, "may I ask a question?"

"Certainly," the rabbi replied. "How may I help you?"

The man began. "I understand that on Passover we are commanded to drink four cups of wine at the Seder in honor of God's promise to free our ancestors from bondage."

"That is true," the rabbi said.

"Here is my question. Can I fulfill the commandment by drinking milk instead of wine?"

"If drinking wine will make you sick or damage your health, you are permitted to drink milk," the rabbi told him.

"There is no problem with my health, Rabbi," the poor man answered. "The problem is in my pockets. Or what is not in them. They are empty.

I don't have any money. I cannot afford to buy wine. But thank you for answering my question. I will find some way to fulfill the commandment." The poor man turned to walk away.

"Wait!" The rabbi opened his purse and counted out ten gold coins. He gave the money to the poor man, saying, "Please accept this money as a gift from me."

"Thank you, Rabbi!" the poor man exclaimed.

"Don't thank me," the rabbi said. "I must thank you. You have given me the opportunity to fulfill another important commandment. All Jewish people are commanded to be mindful of those who might be in need. It is everyone's responsibility at Passover time to make sure that all members of our community have a complete and joyous Seder. Buy several fine bottles of wine, my friend. As you and your family drink the four cups, remember to praise God with gladdened hearts and pray for peace for people throughout the world."

The poor man ran off to the market with a great smile on his face. The rabbi continued on his way home.

When he arrived, he told his wife about his encounter with the poor man. The good woman could not believe her ears.

"You gave a stranger ten gold coins to buy wine? Why did you give him so much money? He could have gotten perfectly good wine for much less. We're not spending nearly that much for wine for our own Seder."

"Dear wife," the rabbi said, "don't you understand? If a man must ask if he can substitute milk for wine, then he probably cannot even afford to buy matzah. I wasn't just giving him money for wine. I was giving him money so that he and his family could have a Seder."

A man raises his wine cup in a detail from a beautiful modern Haggadah created by Polish artist Arthur Szyk. Szyk left Poland before the Nazi invasion. His work became a beacon of hope during the darkest moments of the war. (Szyk Haggadah. London, 1939.)

Urchatz

WASH HANDS

After saying the blessings over the candles and wine, we wash our hands to prepare for *Karpas,* the part of the Seder where we eat a sprig of parsley dipped in salt water.

We wash our hands in a special way. We fill a cup with water from a basin and pour the water over each hand. This is how the priests washed their hands long ago when the Temple stood in Jerusalem.

We usually say a special blessing before washing our hands. This time we don't. We will say the blessing later on in the Seder. Why don't we say it now?

Two thousand years ago, our rabbis thought long and hard about when and how blessings should be said. Some decided that people should wash their hands and say the blessing if they dipped food into a liquid and ate it while it was still wet. In those days people ate with their fingers. Many people shared the sauce in a dipping bowl. Saying a blessing helped everyone to remember to wash their hands.

Other rabbis had a different opinion. Washing hands and saying a blessing before dipping food into liquid had more to do with holiness than cleanliness. It was part of the Temple ritual. Since the Temple no longer existed, they concluded this ritual was no longer required.

The question of whether or not to say the blessing has never been settled. The Haggadah offers a compromise. We wash our hands before dipping the parsley in salt water, but we do not say the blessing. We will say it later, when we wash our hands before eating the Passover meal.

Karpas

DIP THE PARSLEY

After washing our hands, we take greens, usually a sprig of parsley, dip it in salt water, and say this blessing:

בָּרוּךְ אַתָּה יְיָ אֱלֹהֵינוּ מֶלֶךְ הָעוֹלָם בּוֹרֵא פְּרִי הָאֲדָמָה.

Baruch ata Adonai, Eloheinu Melech ha-olam, borei p'ri ha-adamah.

Praised are You, God, Ruler of Creation, who created the fruit of the earth.

We say this blessing before eating plants or vegetables that grow in the ground. Fruit that grows on a tree requires a different blessing.

We eat the parsley immediately after saying the blessing. Parsley is traditionally used at the Seder. However, other vegetables may be substituted. Radishes, turnips, or celery may also be dipped in salt water and eaten. We may use any part of any plant or vegetable that grows in the ground.

Yachatz

BREAK THE MIDDLE MATZAH

There are three pieces of matzah on the table, one of which will be broken to become the *afikomen*. More about that soon. The matzah may be on a covered dish or platter, or in a separate compartment beneath the Seder plate. As mentioned earlier, they symbolize the Kohanim, the Priests; the Levites, their helpers; and the people of Israel. Matzah also represents the *manna* that God provided for the Children of Israel after they left Egypt.

Manna

After leaving Egypt and crossing the Red Sea, Moses led the Israelites through a frightful wilderness. The hungry people cried to Moses. Moses promised that God would send food.

The Israelites awoke the next morning to find the ground covered with a strange golden crust. "This is manna," Moses told them. "God has sent you the food the angels eat in heaven."

Manna was a miraculous food. No matter how much the people gathered, there was always enough for everyone.

Manna had to be gathered early in the morning because it melted away after the sun came up. People could gather as much manna as they pleased, but none could be put away. Stored manna turned rotten. Only on Friday mornings were the Israelites permitted to gather manna for two days. Manna did not fall on the Sabbath. Manna gathered for the Sabbath day did not spoil.

The double portion of manna explains why we have two loaves of challah on the table for the Sabbath and holiday meals. The two golden brown loaves remind us of the double portion of heavenly manna. On Passover, two pieces of matzah take the place of the two loaves of challah. The third piece, the one in the middle, is an extra matzah to be broken and hidden away.

The Falling of the Manna. *The story of the Exodus from Egypt is as important for the Christians as it is for Jews. Numerous masterpieces of Christian art were inspired by the stories of the Old Testament. This particular painting shows the people receiving the gift of manna from heaven. (Giuseppe Angeli [1709–1798]. Church of San Stae, Venice.)*

בתנ֗ה֗צלויקה֗ הנםוישתחוו

שָׁאֲנוּ
אוֹכְלִין
מֵהֶעֲ
שֶׁלֹּא

מצוה

עַל לְשׁוּם
שׁוּם

הַטְפִּיחָן
בְּצֵקָם

Afikoman

The person leading the Seder takes the middle matzah and breaks it in two. The smaller piece is put back in its place. The larger piece is wrapped in a napkin and hidden somewhere in the room. This hidden piece is called the *afikoman*. The children will search for the afikoman later.

The broken matzah that is hidden away symbolizes many things. It calls on us to have compassion for the poor. Poor people make do with crumbs and leftovers. They must always remember to save food for later, for they never know when they will eat again.

Our ancestors in Egypt depended on their masters for food. They ate quickly, hiding away a portion of what they were given. When they left Egypt on the night of the first Passover, they carried their food along, wrapped in bundles and hidden away in baskets.

One hundred years ago, when waves of Jewish people left Europe for America, they carried their food as well. Jewish immigrants could not eat the food served aboard steamships because it was not kosher. They carried loaves of bread and hard-boiled eggs from home to sustain them through the dreary ocean crossing.

We remember our parents, grandparents, and all our ancestors as we break the middle matzah. It is because of their struggles and sacrifices that we are able to celebrate our Seder as citizens of a free land.

Manuscript illumination from the Golden Haggadah illustrating "This matzah that we eat."
(Northern Spain, c.1320.)

Alone in the Castle

BY RACHEL POMERANTZ

Throughout the last 3,000 years Jewish people have managed to celebrate Passover, even in times of adversity. This is a true story of how one Jewish family celebrated its first Seder in America ninety years ago.

Leah stood with her family in the front of the ferry. The salt spray made her sore eyes ache.

"Look, there is the castle!" called her mother in excitement.

"Where?" asked her brother Mendel.

"Do you see the Statue of Liberty? Farther back to the right," explained Mama.

Leah looked past the enormous green woman holding up a torch. By squinting her eyes she could see a red brick building with towers. It did look like a castle, just as Papa had written to them from New York.

"We're getting off soon. Everyone hold on tight to the packages and bundles! If we leave anything on this boat, we will never see it again," Mama warned them.

The new immigrants went down the gangplank to Ellis Island. They were sent to a large room with a high ceiling. Mama settled her family in one corner. Around them, they heard a babble of languages.

"Now, Leah, you watch the children while I try to get our papers in order. I have a list from Papa of just what I have to do." Papa had sailed to America four years earlier, in 1907. Leah, who was twelve, remembered him well. For the youngest children he was only a distant memory. Mama set off with her list.

Mama came back an hour later. "When I told them that Papa had trained as an eye doctor, I saw that they took me more seriously." She looked proud.

"The only thing left is the doctor's examination, to make sure we are healthy enough to enter America," said Mama happily. "Once we get out, we can finally meet Papa. He will take us to Uncle Hyman's house. We might even get there in time to help him search the apartment for *chametz*." *Chametz* is food that contains leavening, like bread and grains. Every speck of *chametz* must be removed before Passover begins.

Leah remembered helping Papa search for *chametz,* walking through the house with a candle and a feather to sweep up the last crumbs. Soon she would be doing it again. Tomorrow night would be Passover.

The medical examination was held on the landing between the first and second floors. The doctor would listen to each immigrant's chest, look down each throat, and then pry up each eyelid. It went fast.

Leah was the last in her family to be examined.

A little girl on an immigrant ship comes to America at the turn of the last century. The Statue of Liberty and Ellis Island are in the upper right corner. (Illustration by Anita Lobel from From Sea to Shining Sea, *1993.)*

The doctor listened to her chest, looked down her throat, and pried up her eyelids. He frowned as he looked into her red, aching eyes. "Quarantine," he pronounced. "Eye infection."

Mama gave a shriek and threw up her hands. Leah would not be allowed to leave Ellis Island because the doctor thought she might have a contagious eye disease. "Don't worry, Leah. We will stay with you. We will go back with you if you have to go back."

Leah knew the rules. The steamship company had to take anyone who wasn't accepted in Ellis Island back to Germany. The ship would sail in five days. If her eyes were not healed by then, their whole dream of joining Papa in America would be ruined. Mama, so happy a few minutes before, seemed to shrink with worry. Her dream of America, the Golden Land, was slipping away.

"No, Mama, no. Take the others and go out to Papa. Maybe the doctors will decide that I can stay. If not, I will go back to Grandma and Grandpa. When Papa has money, he will send me another steamship ticket."

Mama looked at Leah, not sure what to do. "How can I leave you alone in a place like this?" she asked. "I won't be alone," said Leah bravely. "Didn't you tell us that God is always with us?"

Mama, in tears, hugged Leah and kissed her on the forehead. Then she gathered up her bundles. "Come, children," she said wearily, "maybe your Papa will have an idea."

The doctors gave Leah a bed in the infirmary and put some medicine in her aching eyes. In spite of her brave words to Mama, she felt very much alone as she lay down to sleep. She whispered the prayer, *"Sh'ma, Yisrael,"* and felt less lonely.

For breakfast she ate the last of the bread Mama had left her. What would she do on Passover when she could no longer eat bread? Did anyone know about Passover here in the castle?

The woman in the bed on her left was Jewish. Her name was Mrs. Weinberg. Leah explained her fear of being sent back.

"Does your Papa have money for a steamship ticket?" asked Mrs. Weinberg.

"I think so," said Leah.

"If he promises to pay your fare if you have to go back, they may let you stay here to get better. That's what they did for me."

For the first time Leah began to have some hope that she could stay in America. She wished she had some way to tell Papa about this idea. She now told Mrs. Weinberg her other problem. "What can we get to eat on Passover?"

"I hope HIAS will remember to send us matzah."

"Who?"

"HIAS. The Hebrew Immigrant Aid Society. It's an organization that helps people like us, who are coming to America."

So there was someone else besides Mama and Papa who cared about her. Perhaps she could talk to the people from HIAS. They might know of a way for her to avoid being shipped back to Germany.

There seemed to be nothing more Leah could do. She lay down with her eyes closed, hoping that would make them heal faster.

Late in the afternoon, Mrs. Weinberg bustled into the room. "Leah, get up. HIAS did remember us."

"They sent matzah?" asked Leah.

"That's right. The bread of affliction. The bread of redemption. It's a good sign. Better than that, HIAS also sent someone to make a Seder for the Jewish patients in the infirmary. The doctors agreed, as long as he stays in another room. Three thousand years ago God took us out of Egypt and led us into the Promised Land of Israel. Today, in the year 1911, God will take us out of Ellis Island and lead us into the Promised Land of America. Have faith, Leah. Trust in God. It will happen. You will see."

Leah jumped out of bed and put on her best dress. She followed Mrs. Weinberg to one of the side rooms, where a table was spread with paper.

Through the open doorway she saw the Seder table. The man from HIAS had spread a white cloth and set down a pile of matzah. The Seder plate was battered pewter like the one that her family used, and had been set with the egg, the roast bone, the horseradish, the parsley, the charoset mixture, and the bitter herb. Leah sighed. Back home, it had been her job to prepare the Seder plate.

The man was looking in his bag for something else. He straightened up, holding a pile of Haggadot, and Leah got her first look at his face.

The man from HIAS looked directly at Leah. She recognized him at once, even though she hadn't seen him in four years.

"Papa!" Leah shouted. She began to tremble with joy. "What are you doing here?"

"Didn't you get my last letter?" Papa said, just as surprised to see Leah as Leah was to see him. "I work for HIAS here in New York. So many immigrants are kept here with eye problems. Most are not serious. They will clear up in a few days with the right medicine. I talk to the doctors. They listen to me because I know something about eye diseases. The doctors are good people. They don't want to send anyone back, either. Let me see your eyes, Leah. Just as I thought. It is not serious. A few more days and we will all be together again."

Mrs. Weinberg had been right. Matzah truly was the bread of redemption. That's what Passover is really about, Leah thought, as she and Mrs. Weinberg and Papa and all the other Jewish people in the infirmary lifted their wine cups together to say the first blessing.

New life. New hope. New beginnings.

A cozy scene of a family celebrating a holiday was often depicted in American Jewish art and advertising in the early part of the century. (Advertisement for Fischer Russian Caravan Tea, New York, c. 1920.)

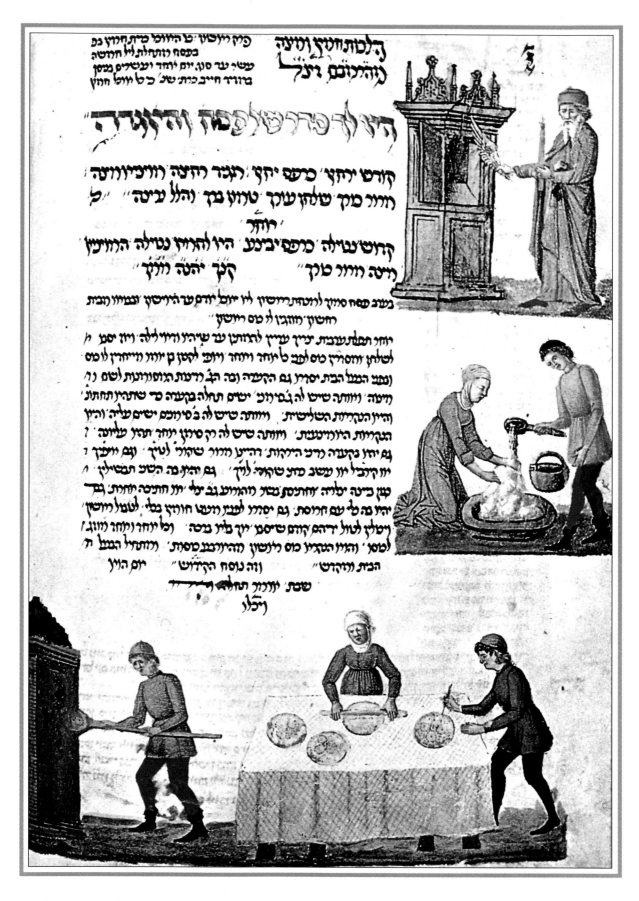

Making Matzah that is kosher for Passover is a complicated procedure. First, a search is conducted for the last bits of leavening. A man looks into dark corners with a candle and sweeps away crumbs with a bird's wing. Below, flour is measured, and the dough is rolled, perforated, and baked. (Rothschild Miscellany, Northern Italy, c. 1470.)

Making Matzah

Most of the matzah we eat at Passover today is baked in large bakeries. In times past every community made its own.

The wheat for the flour used in matzah was grown in special fields. A guard called a *shoymer* watched over it from the day it was planted. The Yiddish word *shoymer* comes from the Hebrew word *shomer*, which means "to guard, to protect." The *shoymer* had to be especially alert when the wheat was harvested, making sure the field was dry so that no moisture got into the grain as it was being stored. Moisture might cause the wheat to ferment, which would disqualify it for being made into matzah.

The wheat was stored and carefully guarded throughout autumn and winter. Thirty days before Passover the process of making matzah began. The local mill was carefully cleaned from top to bottom. The *milner* (miller) ground the wheat into flour. All the kernels of wheat that were not completely crushed had to be sifted out in case they might ferment.

Each household was assigned a day at the local bakery to bake its matzah. Everyone in the family took part so that each person could participate in fulfilling the commandment to make matzah.

BAKING MATZAH

Baking matzah was not easy. The whole process could not take longer than eighteen minutes. The dough had to be continuously kneaded to make sure it did not ferment. Not even the slightest speck of dough could be left on the kneading table. Left alone, it might ferment and contaminate the next batch.

The process of baking matzah began with the *melmayster*, or flour master. He measured out the exact amount of flour required to make one batch of matzah. The *vassergisser* (water pourer) measured out a small amount of cold water and poured it into the flour. The *kneter* (the master kneader) and his assistants mixed the water and flour together by hand to make dough. They did not allow the dough to rest for a moment. After kneading, they divided the dough into the right amount for making one cake of matzah. The kneaders rolled out each portion of dough to the proper thickness.

Then the *redler* (roller) took over. He had a special tool, a *redel*, which looked like a cowboy's spur on the end of a long wooden handle. The sharp points of the spur made rows of holes in the matzah. These holes prevented the matzah from rising while it baked.

Next the *derlanger* (draper) stepped in. He draped each matzah cake over a long rolling pin and carried it to the *shiber*, the matzah baker. The baker put the matzah in the oven to bake. It was

אפיית מצות

THE BAKING OF MAZZOT

customary to kindle the fire in the baker's oven with a dry *lulav* (a palm branch) left over from the holiday of Sukkot. In this way an object that had been used to fulfill one commandment would also be used to fulfill another.

When the matzah had finished baking, it was taken out and given to the *treger* (packer), who packed it up and stored it away until it was time for Passover.

Making matzah required a lot of people. Bakers had to hire extra helpers as Passover approached. This meant jobs for the poor people in town. Their work in the bakeries allowed them to earn money to buy matzah, food, and wine for their own Seders.

Everyone in the community, rich and poor, rejoiced at their Seders, eating the matzah they had helped prepare.

A MATZAH RECIPE

As we have just seen, baking matzah for Passover is a complicated process that must be performed under strict supervision. However, if you want to make your own matzah to better understand how it is done, here is a recipe to try. Make sure an adult is with you because you will be using a very hot oven.

1. Preheat the oven to 550 degrees Fahrenheit for at least 20 minutes.
2. Measure out 3 cups of unsifted flour. Place the flour on a board or flat surface. Slowly add 1 cup of water, kneading it into the flour to make a firm dough. Divide the dough into six portions.
3. Roll one portion into a 7-inch circle. Use a fork to prick holes into one side.
4. Place the rolled-out dough on a cookie sheet. Bake it in the oven for six minutes. Turn it over and bake for two additional minutes.
5. Repeat steps 3 and 4 with the other five portions.

This picture is from a modern pop-up book adapted from The Bird's-head Haggada. *(Southern Germany, fourteenth century.) Again, we see the conical hat, the Judenhut, which was worn by Jewish men to distinguish them from the rest of the population. No one is certain why birds' heads were used. The artist, or his patron, may have wished to comply with the decision of a prominent medieval rabbi, that human faces not be used in art.*

Maggid

TELL THE PASSOVER STORY

Now we come to the main part of the Seder, where we tell the story of Passover. Holding up the matzah so that everyone at the table can see it, the leader recites a famous invitation that begins with the words *"Ha Lachma Anya . . ."*

The words mean: "This is the bread of poverty that our ancestors ate in the land of Egypt. All who are hungry, come and eat. All who are needy, come in and celebrate Passover. This year, here. Next year in Israel. This year as slaves. Next year as free people."

The words of "Ha Lachma Anya" were inspired by a famous rabbi, Rav Huna, who lived in what is now called Iraq during the third century C.E.

Rav Huna was famous for his charity. Whenever he sat down at his table, he would open the doors of his house and cry out for all to hear, "Let all who are hungry come and eat!"

No one is to be hungry on this holy night. No one is to be homeless. No one is to be a stranger. Our doors are open. Anyone wishing to celebrate Passover is invited in.

This ornately engraved Seder plate depicts scenes from the Exodus from Egypt. It also names the Twelve Tribes. The writing is in Hebrew and Arabic. (Gold, silver, and bronze, set in copper. Baghdad, twentieth century.)

The Passover Guest

BY ROBERT RUBINSTEIN

During the Middle Ages, and in some cases well into the nineteenth century, Jews were required by law to live in a run-down part of town called the ghetto. In Venice, this area was located near an iron foundry. Getto *is the Italian word for foundry. It is the most likely source of the word ghetto.*

The children played in the small courtyard of the ghetto. Patches of dried brown grass and broken stone covered the ground. In the middle of this courtyard stood a round, gray, brick fountain. Only no water flowed in it anymore. It, too, was dry, filled with only dirt and brown weeds.

The courtyard was the playground for these children, whose ancestors had been forced to live like prisoners inside the walls of the ghetto right in the middle of the Italian city of Venice. In earlier times, a guard had been stationed at the opening of the alley. At night, the guard would lock a gate, imprisoning the Jewish people. During the day, he would unlock the gate to allow them to go out into the city.

Now there was no longer a guard or a gate. But Jewish people still lived in the old ghetto. And they still had to walk through the narrow alley to reach the city beyond.

Around and around the fountain the smaller children would race. The older children would climb to the top of the fountain's brick wall.

Rachel watched as the older ones balanced on the edge of the bricks. Since she was only five years old, Rachel was too young and too small to walk on the top. But she knew she would do it when she grew

bigger and stronger. The children, even the young ones Rachel's age, would often leave the ghetto's yard to go out with their parents into the streets of Venice. Sometimes, Rachel would be allowed to go with just the older children outside the ghetto.

There were those times, though, when Rachel and some of her small friends didn't ask to leave, but just left without telling their parents. Rachel loved to look in the store windows. She saw all the things that her parents were too poor to buy for her.

To leave this ghetto courtyard, the children had to walk through a narrow, dark passage between two tall buildings.

The moving shadows in the alley frightened the small children.

In this alley also, in the darkest patches of shadow, there often sat a man.

This man would sit in the doorways cut into the sides of the brick buildings. He always wore the same dark, dirty rags for clothes. He never shaved or washed or combed his hair. He'd just sit there some days, sometimes into the nights, drinking from a bottle. His breath and clothes smelled horrible. No one seemed to know where he had come from. He didn't bother the adults or older children when they

passed by, but he often growled at the younger children when they teased him or called him names.

"Dirty old man! Dirty old man! Get out of here!" the children would scream. A few times, they even threw things at him.

He would stagger to his feet, his large body weaving back and forth. He would yell at the children, "Get away! Leave me alone, you little pests!" At times, his voice would change to pleading. "Leave me alone. Let me sit quietly in the shadows. Please." And the children would run back into the courtyard.

But the man never chased them. He never came out from the alley shadows into the courtyard light.

Sometimes, this man would play a nasty trick on the young children. He'd bring a long crooked stick with him. When the children thought he was asleep, they would try to tiptoe silently by him to get to the street.

If he heard them, he would shake his crooked stick at them to scare them. Then he would laugh as the children ran back into the courtyard.

The parents, for some reason, never seemed to become angry enough to chase the man away. "You teased him and fell. What do you expect?" they would say.

It was two days before Passover. Rachel and some of her friends played in the courtyard.

"Let's go to the canals. It's so hot here today!" said Talya, her seven-year-old friend.

"Without telling my mother?" Rachel asked.

"Yes. Let's go now. If we ask, our mothers will only find something for us to do."

And so Talya and Rachel walked across the yard to the opening of the alley.

The two stopped at the alley entrance and peered into the shadows.

"Do you think he's asleep?" Rachel whispered.

Neither one said another word. They watched the shadows silently, looking for some sign of movement from the horrible man who might be in there waiting for them.

"Let's go. It seems quiet enough. He must be asleep, or — or perhaps he's not there!" Talya and Rachel began to walk into the alley shadows. They walked close to the brick wall.

They could see the light from the opening at the other end of the alleyway. Suddenly, they saw a large shadow moving in the alley ahead of them. It was the man. He was coming toward them.

Rachel and Talya turned and fled back into the courtyard. Rachel tripped, scraping her knee and tearing her dress. She cried out.

This time, however, the awful man did not stay in the alley. Instead, he followed Rachel and Talya into the courtyard.

Rachel stumbled again and fell. She lay there on the courtyard stones.

Then, a small woman flew out from one of the apartment doorways. She rushed toward the young girl and the man. Grabbing the stick from the man's hand, she broke it in two and flung the pieces away.

The large man with his dirty beard looked down at Rachel's mother. He gave her an angry look.

"Go back!" Rachel's mother said to the man. "Leave this courtyard. Leave these young children alone! You must never carry a stick with you again! Go now! I feel sorrow for you, but you must leave."

The man hung his head in shame, hurt by these

words. Tears filled his eyes. He turned and slowly moved back into the shadows of the alley.

Rachel's mother shook her head sadly as she watched the man leave. "That poor man. He needs someone to help him." Then, she bent and lifted Rachel into her arms. She brushed away the dirt from her daughter's knee and carried her into the apartment house.

The days passed. It was the first night of Passover.

All day, Rachel and her mother had prepared wonderful dishes, cleaned the house, and set the table for this special night. Even here in the poverty of the ghetto, a new feeling of hope and splendor came into each home with the Passover celebration.

Rachel's father returned early from his work, and bathed and dressed for this special night. Just before the Seder service was to begin, Rachel walked from the kitchen into the living room, where they had set the Seder table.

Sitting at the table was the stranger, the man who usually sat alone in the shadows of the alley.

Rachel ran quickly back to the kitchen. "Mama! Mama! Come quick! The bad man from the alley is out there! The one who scares us, who chases us, is out there! He is sitting at our table, Mama!"

"I know, Rachel," Mama said as she continued slicing carrots.

"But Mama! He is a terrible man! He scared us."

Her mother turned to look at Rachel. "This man is a stranger, Rachel. We Jews have often been strangers in this land. Even here in Venice people treat us as strangers who don't belong. He is here because it is Passover, Rachel.

On Passover we begin the Seder by saying, 'Let all who are hungry come and eat. Let them observe the Passover with us as our guests.' So, we welcome the stranger, especially the person who is alone and lonely."

"But he smells and looks so dirty."

Her mother smiled. "But he is hungry, my child. He is more hungry than we can know, more hungry than just for food. He is alone, very much alone. And he is our guest this night."

"Even though he yells at us and is mean?"

"Yes, even so."

Rachel walked to the kitchen doorway and peeked out.

The man looked the same — yet different. He didn't look so terrible in the soft light, sitting there in her living room. His beard didn't seem so dirty, either. And he had washed his face and hands.

The stranger sat at the table all by himself, alone, his head bowed down. He did seem so alone and sad.

Rachel walked through the doorway into the living room.

The man raised his head. She could see his eyes. They seemed small and filled with great pain.

"Here, Rachel," called her mother. "Put the matzah on the table."

Carefully, Rachel carried the matzah from the kitchen to the table. She put the plate down near the stranger.

And so the stranger came to their Seder table that night and shared the evening with them as their guest. As the night went on, he joined with them in the service, in talking, even in singing the traditional Seder songs.

At the end of the evening, Rachel looked at him and smiled a small smile.

He looked at her. After a moment, he smiled a small smile, too.

After the Passover night, the stranger no longer sat in the alley shadows drinking from his bottle. Instead, he came out into the sunlight of the courtyard. He pulled the weeds out from around the fountain's stones, cleaned the bricks, and repaired things in the apartments for people.

At times, he just sat near the fountain and watched the children play — and he smiled at them.

Indeed, on the day after the stranger had cleaned out the inside of the fountain, the waters returned. The fountain bubbled and flowed with new life.

This illuminated Haggadah depicts a family at the Seder table.
(Rothschild Miscellany. Northern Italy, c. 1470.)

The Four Questions

The wine cups are filled for the second time. The youngest child at the Seder now asks The Four Questions.

מַה נִּשְׁתַּנָּה הַלַּיְלָה הַזֶּה מִכָּל הַלֵּילוֹת?

שֶׁבְּכָל הַלֵּילוֹת אָנוּ אוֹכְלִין חָמֵץ וּמַצָּה, הַלַּיְלָה הַזֶּה כֻּלּוֹ מַצָּה.

שֶׁבְּכָל הַלֵּילוֹת אָנוּ אוֹכְלִין שְׁאָר יְרָקוֹת, הַלַּיְלָה הַזֶּה מָרוֹר.

שֶׁבְּכָל הַלֵּילוֹת אֵין אָנוּ מַטְבִּילִין אֲפִילוּ פַּעַם אֶחָת, הַלַּיְלָה הַזֶּה שְׁתֵּי פְעָמִים.

שֶׁבְּכָל הַלֵּילוֹת אָנוּ אוֹכְלִין בֵּין יוֹשְׁבִין וּבֵין מְסֻבִּין, הַלַּיְלָה הַזֶּה כֻּלָּנוּ מְסֻבִּין.

Mah nishtanah halailah hazeh mikol ha-leilot?
Sheb'chol haleilot anu ochlin chametz u'matzah. Halailah hazeh, kulo matzah.
Sheb'chol haleilot anu ochlin sh'ar y'rakot. Halailah hazeh maror.
Sheb'chol haleilot ein anu matbilin afilu pa'am echat. Halailah hazeh sh'tei f'amim.
Sheb'chol haleilot anu ochlin bein yoshvin uvein m'subin. Halailah hazeh kulanu m'subin.

Why is this night different from all other nights?
On all other nights we eat either leavened or unleavened bread.
  Why do we eat only matzah on this night?
On all other nights we eat many kinds of green vegetables.
  Why do we eat only bitter herbs on this night?
On all other nights we do not dip even once.
  Why do we dip the greens twice on this night?
On all other nights we eat sitting or reclining.
  Why do we all recline on this night?

The rest of the Seder is devoted to explaining why this night is special.

The Original Four Questions

The earliest written version of The Four Questions appears in the Mishnah, the first comprehensive collection of Jewish laws. It was compiled in the third century C.E. by Rabbi Judah Ha'Nasi. Before then, Jewish laws were scattered throughout the Torah and other books or were passed down orally from generation to generation. Rabbi Judah gathered them together in six volumes. One entire section deals with the laws for Passover.

If we look in the Mishnah, we find there are indeed four questions, but only three are ones we still say at the Seder. The fourth question is different:

"On all other nights we eat meat that is roasted, stewed, or boiled. Why only roasted meat on this night?"

The question about sitting and reclining is missing. When and why did the sitting and reclining question replace the one about meat?

A Dutch family making Kiddush at the Seder with their four sons.
(*From* Sefer Haminhagim. *Amsterdam, 1768.*)

Sacrifices at the Temple

Jewish history provides the answer. The question about roasted meat allowed the parents to tell the children about the Passover lamb, which had to be sacrificed and roasted whole. The lamb would be on the table. It had been slaughtered earlier by the Temple priests according to the ritual prescribed in the Torah. The family would eat it as the Passover meal.

After the Romans destroyed the Temple in 70 C.E., the rabbis ruled that sacrifices could no longer be offered. Since a true Passover lamb, which had to be sacrificed in the Temple, no longer existed, there was no need to ask a question about it. Another question took its place — the one about sitting and reclining.

This Passover scene of Hebrews eating the roasted lamb has disturbing undertones. In medieval European tradition, the Passover lamb was seen as a symbol of Christ, whose death was blamed on the Jews. The image symbolically portrays the Jews as having killed this "lamb." Modern Christian leaders, most notably Pope John Paul II, have rejected this belief and expressed remorse for the bigotry and injustice it caused. (Royaumont, Histoire de l'Ancien et Nouveau Testament. France, first printed in 1711.)

A ROMAN BANQUET

Interestingly, the question about sitting and reclining has also become out of date. In the days of Julius Caesar, a Roman banquet was a lavish feast. Wealthy Romans reclined around the banquet table on comfortable couches while their slaves served them.

The rabbis noted the difference between masters and slaves. Masters reclined on couches. Slaves ate sitting or standing. The rabbis decided that the Jewish people would celebrate their Seder lying luxuriously on couches like the citizens of Rome, the masters of the ancient world. For on this night their ancestors in Egypt broke the chains of slavery and became a free people once more.

A Passover Mix-up

A K'TONTON STORY
BY SADIE ROSE WEILERSTEIN

The first story about K'tonton appeared in 1930. Since then, five generations have grown up reading and enjoying the adventures of the Jewish Tom Thumb. Ms. Weilerstein was a pioneer in creating a genuine literature for Jewish-American children.

K'tonton was in Jerusalem. He was spending Passover with the driver Shimshon; his wife, Hannah; and their son, Raphael.

"I don't know how I'd get my Passover cleaning done without K'tonton," Hannah said to Shimshon. "He's a bigger help to me than you are."

"Name one thing K'tonton can do that I can't."

"Can you crawl into the coat pockets to look for crumbs?" Hannah asked. "And he's so good with Raphael."

"Say '*Mah nishtanah halailah hazeh,*' Raphael," K'tonton urged.

"*Abba mah,*" Raphael began. Then he stopped and grinned up at his father.

"That's as far as he'll go," K'tonton explained apologetically. "I guess I'm not a very good teacher. He'll never be ready in time for the Seder." The Seder, the home celebration on the first night of Passover, was only two days off.

"Raphael won't have to ask the *Mah Nishtanah* this year," said Hannah. "We're going to the family Seder. There'll be plenty of cousins to do the asking."

A look of dismay came into K'tonton's face.

"You'll come with us, of course, K'tonton," Hannah hurried to explain. "Did you think we'd leave you behind?"

But it wasn't the fear of being left behind that troubled K'tonton. It was the thought of all the new people he would have to meet.

"Could I go in Raphael's pocket?" he asked. Hannah had made Raphael a new suit for Passover, a real boy's suit with two pockets. "Raphael likes me to be near him. And . . . and . . ." K'tonton blurted it out. "If I went in his pocket, I'd be at the Seder but nobody would know I was there."

"You can go any way you like," Hannah assured him. And that was how the mix-up came about.

The Seder was at Shimshon's father's house. It was a low stone house with a garden in front and a tiled floor inside. When they came in, Shimshon's mother was standing near the long table, arranging

the pillows for his father to lean on. She dropped everything and gave Raphael a warm hug. K'tonton, hidden in Raphael's pocket, could feel the hug. It was just like his mother's. He almost climbed out to wish Raphael's grandmother a happy Passover. Then he looked around at all the aunts and uncles and cousins taking their places at the table, and he was glad he hadn't climbed out. There was a stern-looking uncle in a fur hat and a silk coat. There was an uncle in a frock coat and skullcap, and another like Shimshon in a white shirt and no tie. There were girl cousins and boy cousins. The youngest one was practicing the *Mah Nishtanah* under his breath. The grandfather called him Meirke.

Then the service began and K'tonton forgot all about the company. It was exactly like his father's Seder. K'tonton knew the words so well, he had to be careful not to say them out loud. First the Kiddush, the blessing over the wine; then "Let all who are hungry come and eat"; then greens dipped in salt water. K'tonton managed to nibble a tiny bit of Raphael's.

Then the grandfather turned toward Raphael. There was a twinkle like Shimshon's in his eyes.

"Well, Raphael," he said, "are you ready to ask the *Mah Nishtanah?* You're the youngest, you know."

Everybody smiled. The next minute the smiles turned to amazement. From Raphael's place a voice was rising, thin but sweet and clear: "*Mah nishtanah halailah hazeh mikol halaylot?*" "Why is this night different from all other nights?" Raphael, the *baby,* was asking the *Mah Nishtanah.*

Who had ever heard of such a wonder?

Only Hannah and Shimshon knew that the voice was K'tonton's, not Raphael's. Mind you, K'tonton had not meant to speak. It was just that he was so used to asking the Four Questions. When the proper moment came, he had spoken up without thinking. Now he crouched down in Raphael's pocket, dismayed at the thing that he had done. He wished that he could hide forever.

The family was waiting breathlessly for Raphael to go on. K'tonton could see them through one eye. Clearest of all, he could see Meirke. A tear was running down Meirke's cheek. He had expected to ask the *Mah Nishtanah.* He had practiced it.

Now he can't ask on account of me, K'tonton thought in distress. *And it's his right to ask. Except for Raphael, he's the youngest at the table.*

K'tonton's head was whirling. He looked pleadingly toward Shimshon. Shimshon's lips formed the words, "Shall I tell?"

K'tonton nodded yes.

Shimshon threw him a quick smile, then turned toward his father.

"Father, family," he said, "I am flattered that you think our Raphael is already a *Chacham,* but the truth is that he is still a *She'eno Yodeah Lish'ol.*"

In the Passover Haggadah the *Chacham* is the wise child. The *She'eno Yodeah Lish'ol* is the child who isn't able to ask.

Shimshon continued, "We have a guest at our Seder. It was he who began to ask the questions — by mistake." He lifted K'tonton out of Raphael's pocket and set him on the table. "It gives me great

pleasure to present K'tonton ben Baruch Reuben, a recent arrival in Israel."

A gasp ran around the table. A thumb-sized guest! This was even more amazing than having a baby ask the Four Questions. Every eye in the room was on K'tonton.

But K'tonton was too relieved to mind. Meirke had risen and was asking the *Mah Nishtanah*. Straight through the Four Questions he went, his voice filled with happiness. But not even Meirke was as happy as K'tonton. The wrong he hadn't meant to do had been righted.

K'tonton and his family at the Seder table.
(Illustration by Marilyn Hirsch from Best of K'tonton. *Philadelphia, PA, 1980.)*

A Million Questions (more or less)

A SONG BY LINDA KAUFMAN
AND CARLA SILEN

How does the bread get flat?
How do the fish get round?
Why are we able to sing at the table?
Why do we lie down?

Why does the biggest part
Go to the smallest one?
Why will we eat both bitter and sweet
Before this night is done?

Why was the Pharaoh mean
To the Israelites?
How do you make a stick a snake,
And day turn into night?

How can a fire not burn?
And sea become dry land?
How did a slave become so brave?
Please, tell me if you can.

Why do we say, "Enough,"
Dayenu!
When there is so much more?
Why can't I see the company
That comes in our front door?
It's Elijah!

How much is two *zuzim?*
Where is the matzah hid?
I've got more than questions four.
'Cause I'm only just a kid!

Why on this night do we tell
Of wonders long ago?
Why is this night unlike other nights?
These things I'd like to know.

מַעֲשֶׂה בְּרַבִּי אֱלִיעֶזֶר וְרַבִּי יְהוֹשֻעַ וְרַבִּי אֶלְעָזָר בֶּן עֲזַרְיָה וְרַבִּי עֲקִיבָא וְרַבִּי טַרְפוֹן שֶׁהָיוּ מְסֻבִּין בִּבְנֵי בְרַק וְהָיוּ מְסַפְּרִים בִּיצִיאַת מִצְרַיִם כָּל אוֹתוֹ הַלַּיְלָה עַד שֶׁבָּאוּ תַלְמִידֵיהֶם וְאָמְרוּ לָהֶם רַבּוֹתֵינוּ הִגִּיעַ זְמַן קְרִיאַת שְׁמַע שֶׁל שַׁחֲרִית:

אָמַר רַבִּי אֶלְעָזָר בֶּן עֲזַרְיָה הֲרֵי אֲנִי כְּבֶן שִׁבְעִים שָׁנָה וְלֹא זָכִיתִי שֶׁתֵּאָמֵר יְצִיאַת מִצְרַיִם בַּלֵּילוֹת עַד שֶׁדְּרָשָׁהּ בֶּן זוֹמָא שֶׁנֶּאֱמַר לְמַעַן תִּזְכֹּר אֶת יוֹם צֵאתְךָ מֵאֶרֶץ מִצְרַיִם כֹּל יְמֵי חַיֶּיךָ יְמֵי חַיֶּיךָ כָּל יְמֵי חַיֶּיךָ הַלֵּילוֹת. וַחֲכָמִים אוֹמְרִים יְמֵי חַיֶּיךָ הָעוֹלָם הַזֶּה. כָּל יְמֵי חַיֶּיךָ לְהָבִיא לִימוֹת הַמָּשִׁיחַ:

The Five Rabbis

The telling of the Passover story begins with these words:

עֲבָדִים הָיִינוּ לְפַרְעֹה בְּמִצְרָיִם

Avadim hayinu l'Faro b'Mitzrayim . . .

"We were slaves to Pharaoh in Egypt, but God brought us out of there with a mighty hand and an outstretched arm. If God had not brought our ancestors out of Egypt, our children and our children's children would still be slaves to the Pharaoh in Egypt. Even if we were all wise, intelligent, learned, and well educated in the Torah's teachings, it would still be our duty to talk about our Exodus, or going-out from Egypt. The more any person discusses the going-out from Egypt, the more praise that person deserves."

A FAMOUS SEDER

The Haggadah tells about five famous rabbis who held a Seder in the town of B'nei B'rak. They stayed up all night, talking about the going-out from Egypt. They stopped only when their students came to call them for morning prayers.

These five sages were Rabbi Eliezer ben Hyrcanus, Rabbi Joshua ben Hananyah, Rabbi Elazar ben Azariah, Rabbi Akiba, and Rabbi Tarfon. They lived in Israel during the first part of the second century C.E. The land still bore the scars of the disastrous revolt against the Romans that had taken place seventy years before.

The Romans created one of the world's great civilizations. It was also one of the most brutal. Rome's glory depended on conquest. Its armies crushed anyone who challenged

Here are the Five Rabbis at their all-night meeting in B'nei B'rak. This is from the Leipnik Haggadah, which was created by artist/calligrapher Joseph ben David of Leipnik. He worked in Hamburg and Altona, which belonged to Denmark. The text is in Hebrew, and Seder instructions are in Yiddish. (Leipnik Haggadah. Northern Germany, 1740.)

them. Roman governors extorted heavy taxes and enslaved millions. Slaves, mostly war captives, did nearly all the work in ancient Rome. There were so many slaves and prisoners that the Romans sent them to fight one another in vast arenas like modern sports stadiums. Watching people die was a popular form of Roman entertainment.

Rome occupied Judea, as Israel was then called, in 63 B.C.E. Except for brief intervals, they remained until 640 C.E., when the land fell to invading Arabs. Most Judeans despised the Romans for their violence and cruelty. Jesus of Nazareth was one of thousands of Judeans murdered by the Romans.

In 66 C.E. the people of Judea rose up to fight the Roman invaders. The horrifying war dragged on for seven years. Thousands of people perished. Countless more were sold into slavery. Towns and villages lay in ruins. The Romans leveled Jerusalem. Not one stone of the beautiful Temple remained standing.

The Jewish people might have disappeared forever were it not for these five great teachers and others like them. They refused to surrender to despair. They taught their people that prayer, study, charity, and devotion to the Torah were as pleasing to God as sacrifices in the Temple. God had not abandoned Israel. One day God would send a redeemer, the Messiah, a descendant of King David, to lead them back in triumph to their land and restore the Temple to its former glory.

These teachings would sustain the Jewish people for centuries to come.

Words of Wisdom

The sayings of these five rabbis and others like them are preserved in a book called *Pirkei Avot*. It is one of the classics of Hebrew literature. These ancient words of wisdom still guide us today.

"Cherish your friend's honor as if it were your own, and do not allow yourself to be angered easily." — RABBI ELIEZER BEN HYRCANUS

"Greed, the impulse to do evil instead of good, and unreasoning hatred of others hasten a person's departure from the world." — RABBI JOSHUA BEN HANANYAH

"One whose wisdom exceeds his good deeds is like a tree with many branches and few roots. The wind blows it down easily. But if one's good deeds exceed his wisdom, that person is like a tree with few branches but many strong roots. If all the winds in the world were to blow on it, they could not move it from its place." — RABBI ELAZAR BEN AZARIAH

"God foresees the future, yet human beings are free to choose. God's goodness rules the world; yet all is measured out according to one's willingness to work." — RABBI AKIBA

"You are not required to complete the work of studying the Torah, but you are not free to avoid it." — RABBI TARFON

The Four Sons

Four is an important number in Jewish tradition. In the mystical tradition known as the Kabbalah, four is the number of completion. God's name contains four letters: יהוה. The rabbis of the Mishnah spoke of four kinds of human beings, four kinds of personalities, four kinds of students, four kinds of charitable givers. The number four appears in the Haggadah, too. We drink four cups of wine. We ask four questions. We are told about four sons.

The four sons represent different kinds of people and the ways they learn.

The Wise Son — *Chacham* — is the ideal pupil. He wants to learn as much as his parents can teach him. Parents should take advantage of his eagerness by explaining the history and traditions of Passover, down to the smallest detail.

The Wicked Son — *Rasha* — defies anyone to teach him anything. He asks with a smirk, "What does this mean to you?" "To you," he says. Not "to me" or "to us." He does not consider himself to be part of the Jewish people. The Haggadah tells parents to throw his rudeness back in his face by saying, "We celebrate this Seder because of what God did for *me* when I left Egypt. For *me*. Not for *you*. Had you been in Egypt, you would be there still. God would not have freed you. We would have left you behind."

The Simple Son — *Tam* — is bewildered. He has so many questions, he doesn't know where to begin. He can only stammer, "What does this mean?" The parents should explain the story of Passover to him in simple language. "Once we were slaves in Egypt. God pulled us out of there and made us a free people again. That is why we celebrate the Seder."

And what of the fourth son — *She'eno Yodeah Lish'ol* — the son who cannot even ask the question? Who is this person? He might be a very tiny infant who is not old enough to talk. He might be someone who has lost the ability to speak. He might be an older person, stricken with Alzheimer's disease. These people are part of our family. They belong at our Seder, even if they cannot understand what it all means. We must tell them the Passover story, too, whether or not they can ask the question.

It is interesting to see how each Haggadah is a reflection of its own time. Here, Arthur Szyk interprets The Four Sons as a political commentary on the Jews in Europe before World War II. The sequence begins at the top right and moves right to left. The Wise Son is a traditional rabbinical student; The Wicked Son is an individual who has completely abandoned his heritage; The Simple Son is depicted as one who leads a traditional life and is unconcerned with questions about the modern world; and the one who cannot ask the question is portrayed as a worker trying to choose the right path between modern ideas and the traditional religion. (Szyk Haggadah. London, 1939.)

God's Promise

The Passover story begins by telling how God brought our ancestors out of Egypt, from slavery to freedom.

Who were the ancestors of the Jewish people? Where did they come from? Other cultures tell glorious stories about their ancestors. They were heroes and kings, descendants of gods. They came out of the earth or down from the sky. They were mighty. Heroic. Beautiful.

Not so the Jewish people. We know who our earliest ancestors were. They were people like ourselves, with the same strengths and weaknesses. They weren't kings; they weren't heroes. They were an obscure tribe of wandering nomads who became slaves. In the beginning they didn't even worship God. They bowed down to idols.

History might not know anything about them. There might not even be any Jewish people today were it not for one man. His name was Abraham.

Abraham was the first person to know God. He is not only the father of the Jewish people. He is also the spiritual ancestor of all the Christians and Muslims in the world. Millions upon millions of people in the world today consider themselves to be children of Abraham.

God promised Abraham that his descendants would be as numerous as the stars in the sky, as numerous as the sand on the seashore. God showed him the beautiful, fruitful land of Canaan that his children would inherit. But God also revealed a deeply disturbing future. A time of famine would drive Abraham's descendants, the Israelites, into the land of Egypt. They would serve the Egyptians as slaves.

Abraham asked God, "What good are the promises you made to me if my children are doomed to be slaves?"

God answered, "Do not despair. I will never forget my promise to you. Nor will I abandon your children. They will serve the Egyptians for four hundred years. At the end of that time I will bring them forth into freedom."

We raise the wine cup in memory of God's promise to Abraham. God has never abandoned us. In every age, enemies arise to destroy us, but God delivers us from their hand.

The Promise

LYRICS BY DEBBIE FRIEDMAN

BASED ON EXODUS 6:6, 8:5

This is the promise that I have made to you.

And you will go forth into freedom.

You will be my people and I will be your God.

This is the promise I will keep with you.

And you will go into the land of Abraham and Sarah.

I have lifted up my hand and opened up the way.

That you may live in freedom 'til the end of time.

This is the promise I have made to you.

Family Tree

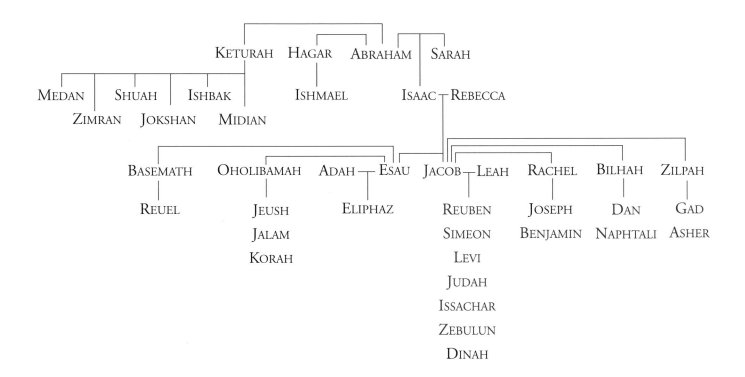

KETURAH   HAGAR   ABRAHAM   SARAH

MEDAN   SHUAH   ISHBAK   ISHMAEL   ISAAC — REBECCA

ZIMRAN   JOKSHAN   MIDIAN

BASEMATH   OHOLIBAMAH   ADAH — ESAU   JACOB — LEAH   RACHEL   BILHAH   ZILPAH

REUEL   JEUSH   ELIPHAZ   REUBEN   JOSEPH   DAN   GAD

JALAM   SIMEON   BENJAMIN   NAPHTALI   ASHER

KORAH   LEVI

JUDAH

ISSACHAR

ZEBULUN

DINAH

This family tree highlights the matriarchs, the patriarchs, and the descendants of Abraham and Sarah.
Abraham's grandson, Jacob, fathered one daughter—and twelve sons, who became eleven of the Twelve
Tribes of Israel. The matriarchs and patriarchs are in red, the eleven of the twelve tribes are in blue. There
is no tribe of Joseph. Instead, two half tribes, Manassah and Ephraim, are named after Joseph's two sons.

The Christian people are spiritual descendants of Israel. Abraham is a forefather of the Islamic people,
through his son Ishmael. Ishmael had thirteen sons and daughters. One, Basemath, married Esau.

Sojourners in Egypt

Abraham had two sons, Ishmael and Isaac. Ishmael's mother was Hagar, an Egyptian maidservant. The Islamic people are Ishmael's descendants.

Isaac was the son of Abraham's wife Sarah, who gave birth to him in her old age. Abraham and Sarah did not want Isaac to marry one of the local Canaanite women. They feared he might be tempted to worship idols, as his brother Ishmael had done. Abraham sent his servant Eliezer to the Syrian city of Haran, where his brother Nahor lived, to find a bride for Isaac. Eliezer returned with Rebecca, the daughter of Nahor's son Bethuel. She drew water for Eliezer and his camels when they first arrived in Haran. Her kindness proved her to be a worthy bride for Isaac.

Isaac and Rebecca had two sons, Esau and Jacob. They were so different that it was hard to imagine they were brothers. Esau was rough and hairy. He lived outdoors, hunting animals and fighting enemies. Jacob stayed home to look after the flocks. He was gentle and soft-spoken.

Jacob became Rebecca's favorite. She decided that he, not his older brother Esau, deserved the birthright, the blessing Abraham intended to pass down to the oldest son of his descendants.

With Rebecca's help, Jacob tricked Isaac into giving him that blessing. Rebecca covered Jacob's arms and neck with goatskins. Isaac, who was nearly blind, felt Jacob's hands and thought he was Esau. "The voice is Jacob's voice, but the hands are Esau's hands," Isaac said. He gave Jacob the blessing anyway.

Rebecca feared that Esau might kill his brother when he learned how he had been cheated. She sent Jacob back to Haran to live with her brother Laban.

Jacob soon learned that his uncle Laban could be even trickier than he was. Jacob agreed to work for Laban for seven years. At the end of that time they agreed he would marry Rachel, Laban's younger daughter. Laban deceived Jacob the way Jacob had deceived Isaac. On the day of the wedding Jacob lifted his bride's veil and discovered he had married Leah, Rachel's older sister.

"It is not our custom for the younger sister to marry before the elder," was Laban's excuse.

Jacob had to work for another seven years before he could marry Rachel.

God blessed Jacob. His flocks and herds increased. He decided to return to the land of Canaan to see if his parents were still alive. Along the way he made peace with his brother Esau and wrestled all night with a mysterious stranger who may have been an angel, or even God himself. The stranger gave Jacob a new name. He called him "Yisra-El," meaning "One Who Wrestles with God." Jacob's

descendants became known as the Children of Israel, or Israelites.

Jacob had twelve sons and one daughter. His favorite child was Joseph, the firstborn son of his beloved wife Rachel, who had died after coming to Canaan. Jacob gave Joseph a beautiful cloak woven with bright colors. His other sons grew jealous. None of them possessed such a fine garment.

Joseph made his brothers hate him even more by telling them about two strange dreams he had. He dreamed that he and his brothers were binding sheaves in a wheat field. Joseph's sheaf stood up. His brothers' sheaves came and bowed before it. Another time, Joseph dreamed that the sun, the moon, and eleven stars bowed down to him.

His brothers became enraged. "Does Joseph think he will rule over us someday?" they asked one another.

Soon afterward, Jacob sent his sons to pasture his flocks in the fields around the city of Shechem. He told Joseph to go after them, to see if all was well. The brothers saw Joseph coming, wearing his cloak of many colors. "Here comes the dreamer," they said. "Let us kill him. We will throw his body into a pit and say that a wild animal attacked him."

Reuben, Jacob's oldest son, pleaded with his brothers to spare Joseph's life. The brothers captured Joseph. They pulled off his cloak and threw him into a pit. As they pondered what to do with him, a band of Midianites came by. These nomads were traders, bound for Egypt. Joseph's brothers sold him to the Midianites. They stained his cloak with goat's blood and took it back to Jacob, telling him that Joseph had been killed.

When Jacob saw the bloody cloak, he believed his favorite son was dead. He wept and wept. No one could comfort him.

The Midianites took Joseph to Egypt. They offered him for sale in the slave market. An Egyptian official named Potiphar purchased Joseph. The new slave's intelligence and honesty impressed Potiphar. The Egyptian appointed Joseph to be his steward, putting him in charge of his household.

Joseph's good fortune did not last. Potiphar's wife fell in love with him. Joseph refused to betray his master. He rejected her advances. Enraged, Potiphar's wife complained to her husband that Joseph had dishonored her. Potiphar did not know whom to believe. He trusted Joseph, but he could not ignore his wife's accusations. Joseph was taken away and thrown into prison.

Among the men imprisoned with Joseph were two important men from Pharaoh's household, the royal butler and the royal baker. The butler had been thrown in prison for spilling Pharaoh's wine; the baker for baking a mouse in Pharaoh's bread. When they learned that Joseph had the power to interpret dreams, they asked him to explain two strange dreams they had recently had.

The butler dreamed that he stood before a grapevine with three branches. As he watched, the vine bloomed and blossomed into grapes. The butler squeezed juice from the grapes into Pharaoh's cup. He brought the cup to Pharaoh, who took it and drank.

The baker dreamed that he carried three baskets filled with bread and cakes on his head. Birds flew down and ate the bread from the baskets.

(Top right) Joseph is being pulled up from the pit as his coat is smeared with blood. (Top left) Joseph is sold to the Midianites. (Bottom right) Joseph's father, Isaac, tears his clothes in mourning when his brothers return with Joseph's bloodied coat. (Bottom left) Joseph with Potiphar's wife. (Below) Joseph interpreting dreams while in prison. (Golden Haggadah. Northern Spain, c. 1320.)

Joseph told the butler, "In three days, Pharaoh will release you from prison. He will restore your honor. You will be his butler again and bring him his cup. Do not forget me. Tell Pharaoh I was thrown into prison, even though I committed no crime."

He told the baker, "In three days' time, Pharaoh will cut off your head and hang your body from a tree. The birds will eat your flesh."

Everything happened as Joseph had predicted. Within three days the butler was restored to his post. The baker was put to death and his body hung on a tree for the birds to eat. But Joseph's hopes were in vain. As soon as the butler returned to the royal palace, he forgot about the Hebrew prisoner who had interpreted his dream.

One night Pharaoh had a dream. He dreamed that he stood on the bank of the Nile. Seven fat cows came out of the river, followed by seven lean cows. The seven lean cows ate up the seven fat cows.

Pharaoh awoke, puzzled by this disturbing dream. After a while he fell asleep again. No sooner had he closed his eyes when he had another dream. He saw himself standing on the edge of a wheat field where seven ripe ears of wheat grew on a single stalk. Beside them grew seven thin, parched ears. As Pharaoh watched, the seven thin ears devoured the seven ripe ears.

In the morning Pharaoh sent for his magicians. He asked them to explain these two strange dreams. No one could give him a sensible answer. At last the royal butler spoke. He told Pharaoh that while he was in prison he had met a Hebrew slave named Joseph who interpreted dreams. Everything that Joseph had predicted had come true.

Pharaoh ordered that Joseph be released from prison and brought to the palace. When he arrived, Pharaoh described his two dreams. Joseph said, "I understand the meaning of your dreams. Egypt will be blessed with seven years of plenty, followed by seven years of famine. All the abundance of the seven good years will be consumed during the seven lean years."

"What must be done to prevent my people from starving?" Pharaoh asked.

"Pharaoh must appoint one man to be steward over all of Egypt. Let him collect one fifth of all the food grown during the seven good years and store it in silos and granaries throughout the land. If this is done, there will be food for all during the seven years of famine."

Pharaoh appointed Joseph to rule over Egypt in his name. Joseph collected grain and stored it during the seven good years. When famine came, there was food to eat in Egypt. The Egyptians praised Joseph, who had saved them from starvation.

The rest of the world was not so fortunate. Even the rich land of Canaan suffered during the seven lean years. Jacob heard there was food in Egypt. He sent ten of his sons there to buy grain. Benjamin, Jacob's youngest son, remained behind. Benjamin was also the child of his beloved Rachel. Jacob still grieved for Joseph; he could not bear to have anything happen to Benjamin.

Jacob's ten sons journeyed down to Egypt. They were taken before Pharaoh's viceroy. They did not realize that the man questioning them was their brother Joseph. But Joseph recognized them.

"Who are you? Why have you come?" he asked.

They answered, "We are twelve brothers, sons of

(Top right) Pharaoh dreams of cows and corn. (Top left) Joseph interprets Pharaoh's dreams. (Bottom right) Joseph orders the arrest of Simeon. (Bottom left) Joseph makes himself known to his brothers and kisses Benjamin. (Golden Haggadah. Northern Spain, c. 1320.)

one father. We have come to Egypt to buy grain."

"I count ten, not twelve. You are lying. You must be spies," said Joseph.

"No, my lord!" the brothers replied. "We are not spies. We are telling the truth. One of our brothers died many years ago. The youngest is home with our father in Canaan."

Joseph ordered his soldiers to arrest them. The brothers remained in a cell for three days. Then Joseph released them, saying, "If what you tell me is true, go back to Canaan and return with your youngest brother. One of you will remain in Egypt as my hostage."

The brothers did not protest. "God is punishing us for what we did to Joseph," they said. They spoke in the Hebrew language, thinking the Egyptian would not understand. Joseph left the room and wept. He rejoiced to see his brothers again and to learn that his father and younger brother Benjamin were still alive. He wondered if his brothers were still the same violent men who had thrown him in the pit. Had they truly changed? Joseph decided to put them to the test.

Returning, he announced his decision. One brother, Simeon, would remain behind as a prisoner. The others were free to buy grain and return home. Joseph gave secret orders to his servants that the gold and silver used to pay for the grain be hidden in his brothers' grain sacks.

On the way back to Canaan, the brothers discovered the money hidden in the grain. They could not understand what was happening. When they returned home, they told their father about the Egyptian official who had taken Simeon hostage and had insisted they come back with

Benjamin. They showed him the money they had found in their sacks.

"First Joseph is gone, now Simeon! And you want to take Benjamin back to Egypt? Woe is me!" Jacob cried. He refused to allow them to return.

Soon they had no choice. The grain from Egypt was gone. The family had nothing to eat. Jacob finally agreed to allow Benjamin to accompany his brothers on a trip back to Egypt. He gave his sons a rich present of gold and spices to give to the Egyptian official. He also told them to return the money they had found in their sacks.

The brothers returned to Egypt. They gave Joseph the gifts they had brought from Canaan, as well as the money that had been returned. "It is yours," Joseph said. "God must have given it back to you. I know nothing about it." He ordered Simeon released. Suddenly, he noticed Benjamin.

"Is this Benjamin, your youngest brother?" he asked. When told that he was, Joseph could no longer control himself. He left the room and wept.

After he returned, he ordered that a banquet be set before the brothers. He gave them all rich presents, but Benjamin received five times as much as anyone else.

When the brothers went to buy grain, Joseph told his servants to fill their sacks and to secretly return their money. However, this time he ordered that his silver drinking cup be hidden in Benjamin's sack.

The brothers were on their way back to Canaan when they saw a troop of Egyptian soldiers coming after them. They asked the soldiers what was wrong.

"Our master was generous with you. Is this how you repay him? By stealing his drinking cup?" the soldiers said.

The brothers denied taking anything. "Search our sacks. If you find the missing cup, you can kill whoever stole it. The rest of us will become your slaves."

"The person who stole the cup will become a slave. The rest can go free," said the Egyptians.

The soldiers searched the sacks. They found the cup in Benjamin's sack.

The brothers threw themselves on the ground, tearing their clothes and weeping. "Woe is us!" they cried. "How can we return home without our brother Benjamin? Our father will die when he learns he is lost." They decided to accompany Benjamin and the soldiers back to Egypt.

Judah begged Joseph to be merciful. He offered himself for punishment in Benjamin's place. It was Judah who had sold Joseph to the Midianites. Now he was offering to become a slave himself for his younger brother's sake.

Love for his brothers overcame Joseph. He ordered all the Egyptians to leave the room. Then he revealed himself to his astonished brothers: "I am Joseph, the one you sold into slavery! It was not you, but God, who brought me here."

Joseph urged his brothers to return to Canaan. They were to bring Jacob, their families, their flocks, and their herds to Egypt. Joseph promised to prepare a place for them to settle.

And so it was that Jacob and his family went down into Egypt, to settle in the land of Goshen. There they prospered and multiplied. However, the Children of Israel did not become Egyptians. They remained a separate people, sojourners in Egypt. They never forgot their homeland in Canaan. Nor did they ever cease worshipping the God of their forefathers, Abraham, Isaac, and Jacob.

The Hebrew Midwives: A Midrash

BY NINA JAFFE

A midrash is a rabbinic legend that expands or explains a Bible story. This midrashic story is based on the book of Exodus 1:15–22.

Many years passed after Joseph, Abraham's great-grandson, brought the Children of Israel down into Egypt. They prospered there for many generations. The old Pharaoh died, and his son took up the golden scepter and sat upon the royal throne. And this Pharaoh grew to fear the Children of Israel. For, he reasoned, "They are many. Their laws and language are different from our own. Someday, an enemy will come to fight against Egypt, and then we will be in danger, for these strange people that live among us might turn against us."

So the Pharaoh spoke with his advisers, and they decided to enslave the Children of Israel and to place taskmasters over them, so that their numbers would grow less and their strength would weaken. At first, when Pharaoh commanded that they build great pyramids of stone, the Egyptians worked together with the Israelites. Then, little by little, the Egyptians left off the hard work and returned to their homes, leaving soldiers with their whips and spears in place as overseers. Now, the men, women, and children of the house of Israel worked alone under the hot desert sun, carrying the great bricks, day after day.

But the people were very strong, and even though men worked from dawn until dusk, and women were forced to carry their young as they climbed the great towers, the people continued to multiply, and Pharaoh grew angry.

So Pharaoh spoke to his advisers again, and they counseled him. "Since the work itself does not diminish them, we must find another way to take their children from this world. Call in their midwives, and we will tell you what to say."

The next day, Pharaoh called in the midwives of the Children of Israel. Their names were Shifrah and Puah. Shifrah was tall and stately. Puah was small and round of face. They wore simple garments of woven cotton as they stood before the Pharaoh.

"Are you the midwives of the people of Israel?"

"Yes, Your Highness."

"Then hear my words. From this day forth, you are commanded to take any male child born and

Workers in Egypt making bricks and mortar around the time of the Hebrew slaves.
(Detail from a mural from a Tomb of the Nobles at Thebes, fifteenth century B.C.E.)

slay him, but the female children you may leave in peace. I have spoken and you shall yourselves be put to death if you disobey my words."

Shifrah and Puah bowed low before the Pharaoh, and walked out of the great hall in silence. But when they reached the edge of Pharaoh's great city, they looked at each other and spoke quietly. They could almost read each other's thoughts, but Shifra whispered them aloud:

"We who are the descendants of Abraham and Sarah — who took strangers in from the desert and gave them drink and rest — are we to obey this wicked command?"

And Puah replied, "We who help bring forth life into the world, do we now become messengers of death? No, it cannot be!" And so they returned to their work, and many new children were born to the mothers and fathers of Israel under their kind and loving ministrations. Now the overseers saw that small boys were still running about in the fields and mud huts, and reported to Pharaoh what they had seen.

Pharaoh called in the midwives before him again, and this time he raised his gold scepter. "Why have you disobeyed me?"

Shifrah and Puah looked at each other. They could read each other's thoughts, but Puah spoke for both of them, her head held high:

"Your Highness, we have tried to obey your command, but it is impossible. These Hebrew women, they are not like the Egyptians. Every day they are at work in the fields — so they are lively and strong as the oxen who pull the great wagons."

"This is true, Your Highness," said Shifrah softly. "These Hebrew women are so strong, they go and

have their babies in the fields. We do not even help them anymore. Their babies are born before we can attend them. So the children come into the world, and we cannot stop them."

Pharaoh was angry with the midwives. Again he commanded that they obey his orders. He did not want to carry out the executions himself, for fear of divine punishment. This time, the midwives left and spoke together again. "If there is a mother who cannot feed her newborn or give him clothing, we will not leave her — for there are women in the villages who have extra cloth and food, and we will ask them for help," said Shifrah. And Puah reached underneath her shawl of woven cotton. "Look what I found in the royal palace, an extra bottle of oil and myrrh. We can use this to wash the heads of the newborn children of our people."

So Shifrah and Puah continued with their work, and finally Pharaoh gave up his commands against them, for each time they appeared before him their answer was always the same, and there was none who could prove otherwise.

And it was said of the midwives, in years to come, that Shifrah and Puah had other names, which were their true names. For the true name of Shifrah was Jochebed, the mother of Moses; and the true name of Puah was Miriam, the prophetess and sister of Moses. But whether we remember them as Shifrah and Puah, or Jochebed and Miriam, their strength and courage live on with us in every generation, for there is a saying in the Talmud: "Had it not been for the strength and piety of the Hebrew women, the Jewish people would never have been delivered from slavery in Egypt."

Moses and Pharaoh

Since the midwives refused to carry out Pharaoh's plan, he ordered his soldiers to do it. Pharaoh commanded that every male child born to an Israelite woman be thrown to the crocodiles in the Nile. Countless Israelite babies met a cruel death before the eyes of their horrified parents. The entire people groaned with misery.

One woman, Jochebed, the wife of Amram of the tribe of Levi, was determined not to lose her baby. She delivered the child in secret. Her daughter Miriam and her son Aaron helped her. They gave the new baby boy two names. Jochebed called him Tuvia, which means "God is good." Miriam called him Jekutiel, which means "I trust in God."

The child was in terrible danger. There were informers among the Israelites, wicked people who hoped to get more food and easier work by spying on their neighbors. One of these traitors would surely hear the baby crying and tell the Egyptians. Before that could happen, Jochebed and Miriam thought of a clever plan.

The two women wove a large basket from reeds that grew beside the Nile. They lined the inside with clay and covered the outside with tar, so it would float. Miriam put her baby brother in the basket and carried it to the river. She put the basket in the water and pushed it into the current. As it floated along, Miriam followed along the riverbank, watching from the reeds.

At noon Pharaoh's daughter came down to the river to bathe. She noticed a basket floating among the reeds and sent her handmaidens to fetch it. To her delight, she found a baby boy inside.

Unlike her cruel father, the kind princess loved children. The beautiful baby touched her heart. She vowed to let no harm come to him.

"It must be a Hebrew child," one of her handmaidens suggested.

"I don't care. I will raise it as my own," the princess said.

"But how will you feed it? It's still nursing."

At this moment, Miriam came forward. She had been hiding in the reeds nearby, listening to the conversation. She told the princess, "I know an Israelite woman who has just given birth. She can be a wet nurse for this baby."

"Bring her to me," the princess commanded.

Pharaoh's daughter gave the baby back to his own mother, Jochebed, who took him home and nursed him until he was old enough to eat solid food. Then she took him to Pharaoh's daughter. The princess became his second mother. She gave him an Egyptian name, Moses, which means "I took him from the river."

Moses found adrift in an ark of bulrushes on the Nile by Pharaoh's daughter. (By French artist Paul de la Roche, 1779-1856, engraved by Edmund Evans in a Sunday magazine.)

Moses grew up in Pharaoh's palace. He was educated to be a prince of Egypt. However, because he remained close to his mother and sister, he never forgot his true identity. He knew he was an Israelite by birth. He worshipped the God of Israel. He felt his people's sufferings as keenly as if they were his own, and hoped for the day when God might show him a way to set them free.

Moses became a young man. One day, he saw an Egyptian beating an Israelite slave. He told the man to stop. When the overseer refused, Moses struck him so hard he fell down dead. Moses buried the dead Egyptian in the sand and drove away in his chariot, hoping no one had witnessed his crime.

Soon afterward, he noticed two Israelites quarreling. Moses told them to stop. They answered rudely, "What will you do if we refuse? Will you kill us as you killed the Egyptian?" Moses realized his secret was known. He had to leave Egypt at once.

Moses fled into the desert. He joined the tribe of Jethro, a desert chief. Moses married Jethro's daughter, Zipporah. His days as an Egyptian prince were over. Now he lived as a wandering shepherd. But he never forgot his people. He continued to worship the God of his ancestors.

One day, while Moses herded Jethro's sheep in the wilderness, he saw a burning bush. Though the bush burned with great flames, it was not consumed.

Moses turned from the path for a closer look. As he approached, God called his name.

Moses answered, "Here I am!"

God continued, "Do not come closer. Take off your shoes, for you are standing on holy ground."

Then God said, "I am the God of your father, the God of Abraham, Isaac, and Jacob. I have seen the sufferings of my people in Egypt. I have heard their cries. The time of liberation has arrived. I will rescue the Children of Israel from the Egyptians and bring them to a land flowing with milk and honey. Go to Pharaoh. I have chosen you to take my people out of Egypt."

Moses was terrified. But God said, "Do not be afraid. Your brother Aaron will go with you. I will give you miraculous signs to show Pharaoh and the Children of Israel. Take your staff with you. With it, you will work wonders before the Egyptians."

Moses returned to Egypt. He and his brother Aaron came before Pharaoh. Moses asked Pharaoh to free the Israelites from work for three days, so they could go into the desert to worship their God.

Pharaoh laughed at them. "Do you think I am a fool? If I allow your people to go to the desert, they will never return. Who is this God you talk about?"

Pharaoh angrily dismissed Moses and Aaron. He decided to punish the children of Israel for listening to these two troublemakers. Up to this time the Egyptians had given the Israelites mud and straw to make bricks. Now Pharaoh ordered that no straw be given. Yet they still had to make the same number of bricks as before.

The Israelites blamed Moses for their troubles. He cried to God, "Why did You send me to Egypt? Pharaoh will not listen to me. Aaron and I have only made the sufferings of our people worse."

God answered Moses, "Do not despair. Go back to Pharaoh. Tell him he must send the children of Israel forth from Egypt. If he asks for a sign, tell

Aaron to throw his staff on the ground. Then Pharaoh will know that I sent you."

Moses and Aaron returned to Pharaoh and told him of God's demands.

"Who is this God of yours? I don't know him," Pharaoh roared. "If you say God speaks to you, show me a sign!"

Aaron threw down his staff. It miraculously became a snake.

"My magicians can perform the same trick," Pharaoh sneered. He ordered his magicians to throw down their staffs. These, too, became snakes. But Aaron's staff swallowed the staffs of the Egyptians.

Pharaoh had no answer for this. Even so, he refused to free the Children of Israel.

Moses and Aaron walked down to the Nile River. Aaron struck the water with his staff. All the water in the Nile turned into a thick, red fluid. So did all the water in Egypt's lakes, pools, and canals. Water stored in jars and cisterns was changed, too. All the water in Egypt had become blood!

Only in Goshen, where the Israelites lived, was there water to drink.

The terrified Egyptians pleaded with Pharaoh to free the Children of Israel. But Pharaoh hardened his heart and refused.

Moses and Aaron returned to the Nile. Aaron stretched his staff over the river. Frogs — hundreds and thousands of them — came hopping out of the water. They hopped into Pharaoh's palace and into the homes of the Egyptians. Every bed, every cupboard, every dish and bowl was filled with hopping, croaking frogs. Pharaoh pleaded with Moses and Aaron to end the plague, but afterward he still refused to allow the Israelites to leave.

God spoke to Moses and Aaron again. He told Aaron to strike the ground with his staff. Aaron did, and a plague of lice rose out of the dust. Lice covered every human being and animal in the land of Egypt. "It is the finger of God!" Pharaoh's magicians wailed. Lice covered them, too.

God struck the Egyptians with plague after plague. Wild beasts followed the lice. They swarmed in from the desert, attacking people in the streets of the cities. Disease struck the flocks and herds. The sacred animals that the Egyptians worshipped died in their temples. A plague of boils broke out. Everyone in the land of Egypt was covered with oozing, bleeding sores. A mighty hailstorm struck the land, smashing the crops in the fields and breaking limbs from trees.

An immense cloud of locusts descended on Egypt to devour what little food remained.

Darkness covered the land for three days. Candles and torches gave off no light. People stumbled about in the darkness, unable to find their way within their own homes.

Each time Pharaoh summoned Moses and Aaron, begging them to halt the plague. But after the plague had ceased, he hardened his heart again. The plague of darkness was the most frightening of all. Pharaoh summoned Moses and Aaron again. This time he was willing to allow the Israelites to leave at once. However, they had to leave their flocks, herds, and all their belongings behind.

"Nothing will remain behind," Moses said. "The Children of Israel must go free with all they possess."

Enraged, Pharaoh drove Moses and Aaron from his presence, vowing to summon them no more.

Exodus. *(David Sharir. Israel, 1967.)*

When I Went Out of Egypt
Grandma Tirzah Remembers

BY GRANDMA TIRZAH

Grandma Tirzah is the pen name of Rabbi David Schaps, who lives and teaches in B'nei B'rak in Israel, where the famous Seder of the five rabbis took place. He based this story on the commentaries and traditions that relate to the first Passover and the Exodus from Egypt. Imagine yourself listening to Grandma Tirzah as she describes the miracles she witnessed when she was a little girl. Ima (pronounced EE-mah) means "mother" in Hebrew. Abba (pronounced AB-ba) means "father."

Oh, children, I could never begin to tell you what that year was like! Of course, you don't know what it's like to be a slave in the first place. May you never know! Ima, my mother, was always tired and bent over, and my father, Abba, was out in the fields working. When we were asleep Ima would sneak out. That was the only time she could visit him.

One morning I heard Ima singing a Hebrew song to herself. It was a song that Grandma used to sing. Our lives were so miserable. I hardly ever heard anyone singing. I asked Ima why she was so happy. Ima told us that God was going to save us soon, that a man named Moses had come and told all the old men about it.

I was just a little girl. I didn't know what she

meant. I knew that we were slaves but I couldn't imagine that our lives would ever be different.

My brother Palti couldn't imagine it, either. "Can we really trust this man Moses?" he wondered. "They say he used to be an Egyptian prince. Maybe Pharaoh is using him to play a trick on us." That made me angry. How could it be a trick? If Ima said God sent Moses to save us, then it must be true. But I never argued with Palti. He was older, and knew so much more.

A few days later I saw an Egyptian woman tiptoe up to the river as if she were afraid of something. She knelt down and took a little sip of water. Suddenly she spat it out. The water was red! The front of her white linen dress looked as if it were stained with blood!

I ran home and told Ima that something was terribly wrong with the river. We couldn't get any more water. All the water in the mighty river Nile had turned to blood. What could we do? Ima smiled and told me not to be afraid. "Go back to the river and get some water, the way you always do. Nothing is wrong with the river. You will see."

I was still afraid, so Palti went with me. I lifted our jug and put it on my head. We walked to the river. Palti helped me fill the jug with water. I lifted it back on my head. Then we hurried home.

I spilled a few drops along the way. But the water wasn't red at all. It was just water.

Palti and I were still wondering what this meant when an Egyptian man came up and snatched the jug away from me. Of course, a man doesn't know how to carry a water jug on his head. He tried to carry it in his arms. The water spilled all over his clothes. But it wasn't water anymore. It was blood!

The Egyptian screamed. He threw my jug into the sand and ran away. Palti and I picked up the jug. We went back to the river and got more water. This time the Egyptians left us alone. As thirsty as they were, they were afraid to come near us.

All the water in the Nile River turned to blood for the Egyptians, although it was still water for us. The Egyptians tried digging new wells. They tried stealing water from their Hebrew slaves. Nothing worked.

More strange things began to happen. If an Egyptian and an Israelite filled their jugs with water from the same tank, the Egyptian drew out blood while the Israelite drew out water. If an Israelite and an Egyptian drank from the same cup, the Israelite drank water while the Egyptian drank blood. Even if an Israelite agreed to pour water for an Egyptian, the water turned to blood the moment the Egyptian touched it.

The only way the Egyptians could get water was to buy it from the Israelites. Water remained water if an Egyptian paid money for it. The Israelites grew rich selling water to the Egyptians. I guess this was God's way of making the Egyptians pay us back for all the years they forced us to work for them as slaves.

"It's a miracle!" Ima and Abba told us. Palti wasn't sure. Believing in miracles wasn't easy for him. "Maybe it's some kind of seaweed that grows in the water and makes it red," he tried to tell me.

And the seaweed goes away for us? I thought. But I didn't say anything, because Palti was my older brother and I never argued with him.

Then came frogs! Millions of them! They jumped all over the Egyptians — in their beds, in their food, croaking all the time. I tried not to laugh at the Egyptians' misery, but I couldn't help

myself. It really was funny! I once saw a frog jump down a man's throat and keep on croaking! The man hit me hard when he saw me laughing at him, but I couldn't stop.

"What's happening?" I asked Palti between giggles. "Why are the frogs acting this way?"

"Maybe something got in the river," was the best answer he could give.

Even stranger things began happening, and this time it wasn't funny at all. When all the cattle got sick and died, we knew that God was punishing the Egyptians. And when the hail broke down their crops and the locusts ate up what remained, we could see the fear in their faces, because their food was running out and they might not have had enough for next year.

Our animals remained healthy. The locusts never bothered our fields.

We thought that nothing bad could happen to a Hebrew, but it turned out that that wasn't completely true. A lot of Hebrews kept asking Moses to leave them in Egypt. They were used to being slaves. They didn't want to be free. Freedom scared them.

Moses never said anything against these people. Their complaints grew louder and louder. They talked about going to Pharaoh and begging him to send Moses away. Then came the days of darkness. All these people suddenly died. The Egyptians never knew, because of the darkness. They never noticed that there weren't as many of us as there had been.

"Maybe this darkness is just a thick fog," said Palti, although he looked as if he were afraid that someone might hear.

Early one evening Ima and Abba told us something important was about to happen; something we would remember for the rest of our lives. We were to stay inside the house all night. We were not to go outside for any reason.

Frogs. *(Michal Meron. Israel, 1995.)*

Abba killed a lamb. He smeared its blood on the entrance to our house. He helped Ima roast the lamb over the fire. Palti and I ate and ate. We never had so much food before. We had never tasted anything so good.

I tried hard to stay awake. I couldn't do it. I found myself growing sleepier and sleepier. My eyes finally closed. I heard something overhead, like a great wind sweeping in from the desert. Did I dream it?

I didn't dream what followed. A terrifying scream! Thousands of voices shrieking all at once!

Abba whispered what was happening. In every Egyptian house, the oldest boy had suddenly died, all at the same moment. Moses had warned Pharaoh, but the Egyptians never imagined it could really come to be. I asked Palti to explain all this, but he just kept quiet and looked scared. Then I remembered. He was the oldest.

We had to leave by morning, but there wasn't much to pack. Palti complained when Ima packed her tambourine. "Why do we need a tambourine in the desert?" he asked her.

"Because I am going to dance," she answered. Then she laughed. I had never seen Ima laugh before. Or dance.

We left Egypt with everything we could carry. Our animals came with us: sheep, goats, cattle. For the next few days we were like a big parade, following Moses and his sister Miriam along the road to the Red Sea.

I heard people in the rear cry out, "The Egyptians are coming after us!" I saw a cloud of dust in the distance. Palti put his ear to the ground. "Chariots! Pharaoh is coming after us with his whole army!"

We stood on the shores of the sea, with the water in front and Pharaoh's army behind. What were we going to do? Then Moses stretched out his hand. He told us to walk into the sea, just like that! With our clothes on and everything.

We did — and the sea split in two before us as we walked across. We didn't even get wet!

My family was near the front, so we couldn't see what was happening behind us until we came up on dry land. There, sure enough, was Pharaoh's army charging right into the sea. The chariot wheels got caught in the mud. The charioteers tried to turn around, but they lost control of their horses. The sea rolled in. The water rose, and soon Pharaoh's mighty army disappeared from sight. Not a single man or animal was left.

God had helped us all this time. We saw it. We saw Him.

Moses sang out a new song. The men echoed the words after him. How exciting it was! Miriam led the women in singing. Ima reached into Palti's bag and took out her tambourine.

My Ima — Ima with the bent back; Ima who never laughed, or danced, or sang — started laughing and singing and dancing with all the other women! And I danced, too. I didn't really know how to dance, but I danced that day!

I wondered what Palti would say about all these miracles, but I never heard a doubting word from him again. God had proven Himself to us. He was our God, and we were His people.

Even me. Even Palti.

In this depiction of crossing the Red Sea, *Miriam and the women play percussion instruments in the front row next to Moses and Aaron. (Manuscript illustration from the Leipnik Haggadah. Altona, 1740.)*

Ten Plagues

We have reached the part in the Seder where we recite the Ten Plagues, in memory of the miracles that accompanied our going-out of Egypt.

As we recite each plague, we dip our little finger into our cups and leave a drop of wine on our plates. This reminds us not to make light of the sufferings of the Egyptians. As the Israelites danced and sang on the shores of the Red Sea after they had safely crossed over, God stopped the angels from joining them in the song of rejoicing. God asked the angels, "How can you sing when the Egyptians, the living creatures I created, are drowning?"

This is why we remove wine from our cups. We diminish the joy of our celebration to show regret for the sufferings of our enemies.

The rabbis point out that the Ten Plagues of Egypt represent justice, not

1. Blood / Dam / דָם

2. Frogs / Tzefardeah / צְפַרְדֵעַ

The Ten Plagues. (Kafra Haggadah. New York, 1949.)

vengeance. Each plague is more severe than the one before. God is warning the Egyptians to free the Israelites to avoid further suffering. The Egyptians were willing. It was Pharaoh, their leader, who hardened his heart and refused. How many times in history has a nation been led into misery because of the stubbornness of its leaders? Think of Germany under Adolf Hitler, or Iraq under Saddam Hussein.

We often create our own plagues. By cutting down rain forests and using fossil fuels wastefully, we cause changes in the earth's climate. Scientists have warned about global warming for years. No one has seriously tried to do anything about it. Now we may be seeing its effects in floods, blizzards, and hurricanes. Did God send these plagues, or did we create them ourselves?

Why did God inflict these particular plagues on Egypt? Each one, the rabbis tell us, is punishment for a specific hardship inflicted on the Israelites. The Egyptians forced the Israelites to draw water for them; all the water in Egypt was turned to blood. They forced them to make bricks to build cities; hailstones the size of bricks fell from the sky. They made them herd cattle and work in the fields; all the cattle died and locusts ate the crops. Pharaoh condemned the Hebrew male infants to death; his own son and all firstborn

3. Lice / Kinim / כִּנִּים

4. Wild Beasts / Arov / עָרוֹב

5. Cattle Disease / Dever / דֶּבֶר

6. Boils / Sh'chin / שְׁחִין

7. Hail / Barad / בָּרָד

males in the land of Egypt perished. God's justice is harsh, but it is always fair. The sufferings of the Egyptians exactly equaled the sufferings they had inflicted on the Children of Israel.

It is important to remember the plagues. For as God judged the Egyptians, so will God judge Israel and all the nations of the world.

We recite the plagues together. Using our little finger, we remove a drop of wine from our cups as we name each plague.

Don't put the wine cups aside. We still have more drops to dip from our cups. Rabbi Judah, a great teacher who lived in the second century C.E., invented an acronym to help us remember the names of the plagues in their correct order.

An acronym is a nonsense word made up of the first letters of words you want to remember. To give an example, one way to remember the colors of the rainbow is to think of ROY G BIV. There is no such person. The letters of Roy's name correspond to the first letters of the rainbow's colors: Red, Orange, Yellow, Green, Blue, Indigo, and Violet.

The Hebrew language uses this device frequently. Rabbi Shlomo Itzhaki, a great medieval sage, is

known by the initials of his name: RaSHI. The Baal Shem Tov, who founded the Hasidic movement at the end of the eighteenth century, is often called the BeSHT, after the three initials of his title.

Rabbi Judah took the first Hebrew letter of each plague and made three nonsense words. The first two words contain three letters. The third has four, adding up to ten. They look like this in Hebrew script. Remember, Hebrew is read from right to left.

דְּצַ"ךְ   עֲדַ"שׁ   בְּאַחַ"ב

Acronyms were important in the days before books were common. Even though every family now has its own Haggadah, we still recite the three words of Rabbi Judah's acronym and dip our pinkies to remove a drop of wine for each. In this way we make sure we haven't left out any of the plagues. We recite with Rabbi Judah:

D'tzach.   Adash.   B'achav.

(D tza ch A da sh B' a ch av are the phonetic sounds that begin each plague. The last "B" in this acronym has become a "V.")

8. Locusts / Arbeh / אַרְבֶּה

9. Darkness / Choshech / חֹשֶׁךְ

10. Killing the Firstborn / Makkat Bechorot / מַכַּת בְּכוֹרוֹת

How Many Plagues?

A PLAY BY ERIC A. KIMMEL

RABBI YOSÉ

I can prove that if the Egyptians suffered ten plagues in Egypt, they suffered fifty at the Red Sea.

RABBI ELIEZER AND RABBI AKIBA

How so?

RABBI YOSÉ

Remember when Aaron threw down his staff and it became a snake? Pharaoh's magicians said, "It is the *finger* of God!" At the Red Sea, the Torah says, "Israel saw the great hand of God raised against the Egyptians." Now, if the finger of God can cause ten plagues, God's whole hand, which has five fingers, must have caused fifty plagues.

RABBI ELIEZER

That's very good. I can do even better. When the Book of Psalms speaks about the plagues, it says: "God sent upon them blazing anger: wrath, fury, trouble, and legions of destroying angels."

The plagues, like God's blazing anger, consisted of four parts: (1) wrath, (2) fury, (3) trouble, and (4) legions of destroying angels. Since each plague was actually four plagues, the Egyptians must have suffered forty plagues in Egypt, not ten. And if God's finger could cause forty plagues, all five fingers of God's whole hand must have caused two hundred. Therefore, the Egyptians suffered forty plagues in Egypt and two hundred at the Red Sea. What do you think of that?

RABBI AKIBA

Plagues, shmagues! Do you want to talk about plagues? I'll give you plagues! I can prove that the Egyptians suffered fifty plagues in Egypt and two hundred and fifty at the Red Sea!

RABBI YOSÉ AND RABBI ELIEZER

How can you do that?

RABBI AKIBA

Listen closely and you will learn something. I will use your verse, Rabbi Eliezer. You have come close, but your interpretation doesn't go far enough. What does the Book of Psalms say? "God sent upon them blazing anger, wrath, fury, trouble, and legions of destroying angels." I read this verse differently. Each plague was really five plagues, not four: (1) blazing anger, (2) wrath, (3) fury, (4) trouble, and (5) legions of destroying angels. Therefore, I say that if God's finger could cause fifty plagues in Egypt, God's whole hand must have caused two hundred and fifty at the Red Sea.

RABBI YOSÉ AND RABBI ELIEZER

Bravo, Rabbi Akiba! You have proved again that you are our master.

RABBI AKIBA

My dear friends, why are we talking about plagues? Instead of worrying about how many times God punished our enemies, we should be remembering how many times God has blessed us.

Dayenu

The Haggadah is full of rousing songs. "Dayenu" is one of the most popular. It first appears in one of the earliest Haggadot, that of Rabbi Saadiyah Gaon, which was compiled in Baghdad in the ninth century. That means it comes from the same place and time as the stories of The Arabian Nights. It is at least a thousand years old. Dayenu means "It would have been enough." We praise God for all the blessings God has given us. Even if He had only given us just one of these, it would have been enough.

Ilu hotzi hotzianu
Hotzianu miMitzrayim
Hotzianu miMitzrayim
Dayenu

Had God only taken us
Out of Egypt —
It would have been enough.

CHORUS: DA-DA-YENU

Ilu natan natan lanu
Natan lanu et haShabat
Natan lanu et haShabat
Dayenu

Had God only given us
The Sabbath —
It would have been enough.

CHORUS

Ilu natan natan lanu
Natan lanu et haTorah
Natan lanu et haTorah
Dayenu

Had God only given us
The Torah —
It would have been enough.

CHORUS

Here Moses receives the Torah on Mount Sinai and passes it on to the people.
(Regensburg Pentateuch. South Germany, early fourteenth century.)

And You Shall Teach Your Children

BY GERSHON LEVINE

Gershon Levine based this story on his own experiences fighting for Soviet Jews in the 1960s.

"Where is your father?"

Grandma was getting antsy. The table was set, the food was cooked, and we were about to start the Seder. Dad, however, was missing. Mom walked over to the staircase and shouted, "Avi, if the turkey is dry, it'll be your fault! Let's start!" Suddenly, we heard marching feet on the staircase and a great voice boomed out:

"ONE, TWO, THREE, FOUR, OPEN UP THE IRON DOOR! FIVE, SIX, SEVEN, EIGHT, LET MY PEOPLE EMIGRATE!"

There, at the foot of the stairs, was Dad, shouting into a bullhorn. He was wearing an ill-fitting blue-and-white-striped prison uniform adorned with colorful buttons that had slogans such as: FREE SOVIET JEWS; UP AGAINST THE WALL, MOTHER RUSSIA; NEVER AGAIN; and LET MY PEOPLE GO. The last button had a white Jewish star entangled with a thick chain, which was secured with a thick padlock. The keyhole was in the shape of a hammer and sickle. My baby sister pointed and laughed. Mom rolled her eyes, and Grandma said,

"Oh my God, how long has it been?"

"Twenty-five years," he said.

I turned to Grandma. "What do you mean? What happened twenty-five years ago?"

She answered, "On the night of the first Seder, I sat in the Midtown South Police Precinct with pot roast in my lap so your father would have kosher for Passover food to eat in jail!"

"Way to go, Dad! What did you do?"

He saw that I was aching to hear the story. "My friends and I held a 'Freedom for Soviet Jewry' Seder in Upper Manhattan. But we'll get to that later." He clapped his hands. "*Nu*, let's start our Seder."

Mom recited the Kiddush, we washed our hands, dipped the greens, broke the matzah, and Grandma hid the *afikoman*. After the Four Questions, Mom and Dad told the Passover story in their usual dramatic fashion with props — rubber frogs flew everywhere and Ping-Pong balls bounced like hail. We sang, ate well, and the three hours passed quickly. After the baby was put to bed, Dad sat Mom, Grandma, and me

This white star of David, shackled with a heavy chain and padlock, symbolized the struggle for religious freedom for the Soviet Jews. (Logo from the Long Island Committee for Soviet Jewry.)

on the couch. He put a photo album in my lap.

"Open it."

I flipped through the book. Pasted across the pages were black-and-white photos of long-haired, denim-wearing teenagers — boys and girls holding signs, looking angry and shouting at the camera. There were also newspaper articles about demonstrations and sit-ins from a variety of New York newspapers. One headline read: FIFTY ARRESTED AT SOVIET MISSION! NY MOSES TO RUSSIAN PHARAOH: "LET MY PEOPLE GO!!" Under the headline was a grainy picture of several New York City policemen dragging a burly teen with long, bushy hair into a police van. He was dressed in a striped prison uniform.

"Dad, that's YOU!"

"Yep, though I'll tell you — I was more afraid of Grandma's reaction than of being in jail!" Dad sat back against the couch and chuckled softly to himself.

"Why'd you do it? Why did you get arrested?" I asked.

Dad stopped smiling. He looked soberly at Mom and Grandma and said, "Because Uncle Berl and Aunt Shayne couldn't."

"Who were they?" I asked.

Grandma answered, "My father's brother and his family. They perished during the Holocaust. You know, if my parents hadn't fled from Russia in the twenties they would have been wiped out by the Nazis along with the other six million Jews they killed."

Mom put her hand on Grandma's shoulder and continued, "We were lucky. Our families came to America. Some of the other Jews who lived in Eastern Europe during the war fled deeper into Russia to escape the Nazis and they survived the Holocaust. By the seventies three million Jews lived behind the Iron Curtain in the Soviet Union and Eastern Europe. And they were not allowed to openly practice their Judaism."

Grandma continued, "Right after the Six-Day War between Israel and her Arab neighbors, thousands of young Russian Jews became aware of their Jewishness because of Israel's victory. They wanted to practice freely as Jews or go to Israel. When they applied to leave, they lost their jobs, were investigated by the K.G.B., the secret police, and were refused permission to leave anyway. That's how they got stuck with the name 'refuseniks.'"

Dad stood and paced the room. "The news media thought the whole Soviet Jewry issue was boring — a real snoozefest, relegated to page nine of the newspapers or somewhere between weather and sports on TV. People's lives were on the line and we had to ensure that the plight of Soviet Jews made it to page one and the lead story on the evening news. We decided to hold a large rally for Soviet Jewry in the form of a Passover Seder, on the first night of Pesach, right on the Russians' doorstep in New York City, at the Soviet mission to the United Nations!

"Ten of us wore these uniforms as a visual representation of imprisoned Russian Jews. We had to hold our freedom Seder while walking

During the Seder many periods of Jewish persecution are remembered: the slavery in Egypt, the Spanish Inquisition, and, more recently, the Nazi Holocaust of World War II. This Haggadah commemorates the Egyptian enslavement through the metaphor of a concentration camp.
(Munich Haggadah, Noar Halutzi Edition. Germany, 1948.)

around in a circle, because if we stopped, the police could arrest us for loitering. So, we walked and asked the Four Questions. We walked and drank the four cups of wine. We walked and told the story of the Exodus from Egypt. All the while, people joined the rally and we eventually had to stop walking because our numbers grew to about four hundred. The newspapers and TV crews were out in full force because of the novelty of us holding a Seder at the Russian mission.

"When we shouted, the canyons of New York's East Side shook with our voices. With the cameras rolling, I climbed on a mailbox, held the bullhorn to my mouth, and shouted, 'Am Yisrael Chai! The people of Israel live! Six million never again! Let my people go! Let my people go! Let my people go!'

"At that point the whole crowd was yelling and chanting and moving close to the police barricades. When I yelled, 'Shlach et ami!' which is Hebrew for 'Let my people go!', the crowd rushed the police line protecting the Soviet mission, almost

as if it was a prearranged signal. While many demonstrators struggled with the police, others sat down in the street to block traffic. At the height of the chaos, the ten of us dressed in prison uniforms pulled out handcuffs and chained ourselves to the fence of the mission.

"Many were injured scuffling with the police and taken to the hospital. But the news crews broadcast my words around the world:

"'According to Soviet law, holding a Seder is a crime! Baking matzah is a crime! My Uncle Berl and Aunt Shayne aren't here today — they perished in Auschwitz. But my cousins Boris and Svetlana are calling out to me — to hold the Seder they cannot have! On this night, when we celebrate the greatest of freedoms, the Exodus from Egypt, three million Jews toil and suffer in Russian slavery! Six million Jews perished in the Holocaust and no one raised a voice while Hitler's ovens burned. Tonight we raise voices and our fists to free enslaved Jews!'

"When the smoke cleared, we ended up in jail, and Grandma and other parents sat in the lobby of the precinct to bail out their kids. New York's mayor held a press conference condemning our actions, but he warned the Soviet Union that all law-abiding citizens would keep watch how Russian Jews were treated. Our Seder had worked. On that Passover night, freedom for Soviet Jews was a front-page issue!"

Dad's face was flushed with excitement and he slumped back on the couch after telling the story.

"The Passover Seder is more than a great story with a tasty meal. We act it out year after year as a reminder of our freedom. The Jewish people still have plenty of enemies. It *should* make us uncomfortable to know that we are free while others are in danger. There comes a time when you say '*dayenu*'— enough is enough. There comes a time in your life when you have to take a stand for something you believe in."

Dad took off the prison uniform, folded it into a tight package, and handed it to me. "We suffered as slaves for many years and that taught us never to accept injustice. God took us out of Egypt with a mighty outstretched arm in order to receive the Torah at Mount Sinai. That should have been enough — *dayenu* — but it wasn't enough. The Torah commands us to act: *Tzedek, tzedek tirdof.* Justice, justice shalt thou pursue!" He placed the uniform in my hands. "Well, kid, it's your bar mitzvah year. The uniform doesn't fit me anymore. It's yours now."

Dad grabbed my hand, scooped me into a bear hug, and whispered into my ear: "*Tzedek, tzedek tirdof.* What justice are you going to pursue?"

Pesach, Matzah, Maror

THE PASSOVER LAMB,
THE UNLEAVENED BREAD,
THE BITTER HERB

Rabbi Gamaliel the Elder was a great sage who lived during the first century C.E. when the Temple stood in Jerusalem. As head of the Sanhedrin, the religious council of Judea, he was the spiritual leader of Jews throughout the world.

Rabbi Gamaliel is an important person for Christians as well. He may have known Jesus and Saint Paul. Saint Paul claims to have been one of his students. There is no reason to doubt this. A great teacher like Gamaliel welcomed all who came to study. Jesus may have discussed religious matters with him.

Rabbi Gamaliel protected the first Christians from those who wanted to attack them. "If God does not approve this new belief, it will disappear by itself," he argued. "It is unjust to persecute these people."

Rabbi Gamaliel ruled that the telling of the Passover story was not complete unless the leader and the guests had discussed three things:

Pesach (the Passover lamb), Matzah (the unleavened bread), and Maror (the bitter herb).

First, the leader holds up the shank bone, symbolizing the Passover lamb. The Passover sacrifice of the lamb reminds us that God "passed over" the houses of our ancestors on the night when the Egyptian firstborn were struck down.

Next, the leader holds up the middle matzah, symbolizing the unleavened bread that our ancestors carried with them as they began their journey to freedom. The matzah reminds us that the dough our ancestors carried with them did not have time to rise because of the haste in which they left Egypt.

Last, the leader holds up the bitter herb, symbolizing the sufferings of our ancestors. The maror reminds us how embittered the lives of our ancestors were when they lived in Egypt.

The rabbis ask: Shouldn't we talk about maror first? In the Passover story, our ancestors' lives became embittered. Then they baked unleavened bread. The Passover sacrifice came last, just before God came down to Egypt and set them free. Why did Rabbi Gamaliel reverse the order?

Here is the answer: We never fully understand the bitterness of slavery until we are set free. Our ancestors in Egypt were born as slaves. They had never experienced freedom. They could not really understand the true bitterness of slavery until God delivered them.

This is why Rabbi Gamaliel put Pesach first. The Passover lamb represents liberation. We cannot fully taste slavery's bitterness until we first know what it means to be free.

In every age, in every generation, we must see ourselves as if we, personally, had been brought out of Egypt. We must say to our children, "This is what God did for ME when I left Egypt." For it was not only our ancestors, but we ourselves whom God freed from slavery.

Therefore, we lift our wine cups and praise God, the Redeemer of Israel, as we say the blessing over the second cup of wine.

בָּרוּךְ אַתָּה יְיָ אֱלֹהֵינוּ מֶלֶךְ הָעוֹלָם בּוֹרֵא פְּרִי הַגָּפֶן.

Baruch ata Adonai, Eloheinu Melech ha-olam, borei p'ri ha-gafen.

Praised are You, God, Ruler of Creation, who created the fruit of the vine.

Kadish D'rabanan

LYRICS BY DEBBIE FRIEDMAN

In the synagogue, different forms of the Kadish prayer are used to mark the ending of one part of the service and the beginning of the next. The word Kadish means "sanctification." The Kadish D'rabanan is recited at the end of the Torah service to honor teachers, students, and all who study God's words. Debbie Friedman, one of America's foremost contemporary Jewish singers and songwriters, has written this beautiful version of the Kadish D'rabanan. Since we have come to the end of the Maggid portion of our Seder, and since we have been studying the story of Passover, one of the most important parts of the Torah, let us now join together to sing in praise of teachers and students.

For our teachers and their students
And the students of the students.
We ask for peace and loving kindness,
And let us say: Amen.

And for those who study Torah,
Here and everywhere,
May they be blessed with all they need,
And let us say: Amen.

We ask for peace and loving kindness.
And let us say: Amen.

This unusual picture shows women studying with men. Most medieval Jewish women were not encouraged to study. Medieval nuns, however, who had time to study and no family responsibilities, were often highly learned. It is possible this picture was painted by a Christian artist who was more accustomed to seeing women with books. It may also be that this manuscript was commissioned by a wealthy, literate Jewish Woman. And there are some who believe this was executed by a woman artist. (Darmstadt Haggadah. Germany, fifteenth century.)

Rachtzah

WASH HANDS AND SAY THE BLESSING

We are almost ready for the Passover meal. We wash our hands again, saying the blessing this time:

בָּרוּךְ אַתָּה יְיָ אֱלֹהֵינוּ מֶלֶךְ הָעוֹלָם אֲשֶׁר קִדְּשָׁנוּ בְּמִצְוֹתָיו וְצִוָּנוּ עַל נְטִילַת יָדָיִם.

Baruch ata Adonai, Eloheinu, Melech ha-olam, asher kid'shanu b'mitzvotav v'tzivanu al n'tilat yadayim.

Praised are You, God, Ruler of Creation, who has made us holy through Your commandments, and commanded us to follow the ritual of washing our hands.

From this point on, there must be no unnecessary talking or interruption until all the blessings preceding the Passover meal are completed.

Motzi Matzah

SAY THE BLESSINGS, EAT THE MATZAH

The leader lifts the two whole matzot with the piece of broken matzah in between and says the blessing for the bread:

בָּרוּךְ אַתָּה יְיָ אֱלֹהֵינוּ מֶלֶךְ הָעוֹלָם הַמּוֹצִיא לֶחֶם מִן הָאָרֶץ.

Baruch ata Adonai, Eloheinu, Melech ha-olam, ha-motzi lechem min ha-aretz.

Praised are You, God, Ruler of Creation, who brings forth bread from the earth.

The leader puts down the bottom matzah. Holding up the top and middle matzot, he says a special blessing for matzah:

בָּרוּךְאַתָּה יְיָ אֱלֹהֵינוּ מֶלֶךְ הָעוֹלָם אֲשֶׁר קִדְּשָׁנוּ בְּמִצְוֹתָיו וְצִוָּנוּ עַל אֲכִילַת מַצָּה.

Baruch ata Adonai, Eloheinu, Melech ha-olam, asher kid'shanu b'mitzvotav v'tzivanu al achilat matzah.

Praised are You, God, Ruler of Creation, who has made us holy through Your commandments and commanded us concerning the eating of matzah.

The leader breaks the top and bottom matzot, the two unbroken pieces, into bits. He gives the guests at the Seder table a piece from each. Each person must eat at least enough matzah to equal the size of an olive.

The two pieces of matzah must be eaten plain. Not even salt may be added. Eating matzah is a holy commandment. Nothing should disguise or alter its taste.

Maror

DIP THE BITTER HERB

The leader now takes pieces of bitter herb and dips them into charoset, the sweet wine, fruit, and nut mixture. How much maror do we have to eat? The rule again is "equal to an olive." It may be a small olive.

The leader distributes the maror around the Seder table. The sweetness of the charoset removes some of the bitterness, but must not disguise it completely. Slavery is bitter, not sweet. The point of eating maror is to taste that bitterness. This is the reason why we are also not permitted to swallow maror in one gulp, like bad-tasting medicine. We must chew it, to fully experience its sharp bite, like the bit in a horse's mouth. This is what it is like to be a slave: to have a master on your back, making you do as he wishes, enforcing his orders with bridle, spur, and whip.

The leader says the blessing. Together we eat maror.

בָּרוּךְ אַתָּה יְיָ אֱלֹהֵינוּ מֶלֶךְ הָעוֹלָם אֲשֶׁר
קִדְּשָׁנוּ בְּמִצְוֹתָיו וְצִוָּנוּ עַל אֲכִילַת מָרוֹר.

Baruch ata Adonai, Eloheinu Melech ha-olam asher kid'shanu b'mitzvotav v'tzivanu al achilat maror.

Praised are You, God, Ruler of Creation, who has made us holy through Your commandments and commanded us concerning the eating of bitter herbs.

Korech

MAKE HILLEL'S SANDWICH

The part of the Seder known as *Korech* follows. The leader breaks the third matzah into pieces and makes little sandwiches by putting one piece of maror between two pieces of matzah. These sandwiches, called *korech*, are distributed to the guests. They dip them in charoset and eat them all at once after saying:

"We follow this ritual in memory of what Hillel used to do at the time when the Temple still existed. During the time of the Temple, Hillel would combine matzah and maror, and eat them all together. Thus he fulfilled the words of the Torah, which say, 'They will eat it together with matzah and bitter herbs.'"

Eat what with matzah and bitter herbs? The missing word is *Pesach*, the Passover lamb. The second sentence should actually read: ". . . Hillel would combine Pesach, matzah, and maror, and eat them all together."

Rabbi Hillel is one of the most beloved and honored figures in Jewish history. This great teacher and sage lived during the early part of the first century C.E.

Hillel taught his students that "together" meant "all at once." Accordingly, he put bits of Passover lamb and maror between two pieces of matzah and ate them together.

We do the same today, or as much as we can. We cannot make korech sandwiches the way Hillel did, because we no longer have a real Passover lamb. All Jewish sacrifices ended when the Romans destroyed the Temple in 70 C.E. Since we no longer have a Temple or a Passover lamb, this part of the Haggadah no longer mentions the word *Pesach*. The modern Hillel sandwich is strictly vegetarian.

Shulchan Orech

ENJOY THE PASSOVER MEAL

The Passover meal usually begins with a serving of hard-boiled eggs in a dish of salt water. Like the egg on the Seder plate, these eggs are both symbols of mourning and of new life. The salt water also has a double meaning. It represents the tears our ancestors shed in Egypt. And, it reminds us of the crossing of the Red Sea, when God parted the waters.

Some people may avoid dairy products entirely during Passover. This is because many dairy products, such as yogurt and cheese, are produced by curdling, which is a kind of fermentation. Nowadays, it is possible to obtain dairy products that are certified to be kosher for Passover, but in the past these foods were hard to find and very expensive. Most families solved the problem by avoiding dairy foods altogether.

Some families do not serve lamb or any roasted or broiled meat since an actual Passover lamb can no longer be properly sacrificed. Other families do the opposite. They make a point of serving roasted meat, especially lamb, at the Passover meal, in memory of the ancient sacrifice that their ancestors brought to the Temple in Jerusalem.

There are also regional differences. Sephardic families are more likely to serve lamb than Ashkenazic families. Sephardim are descendants of Jews who once lived in Spain. Many now live in Israel, North Africa, and the countries of the Middle East, where lamb is commonly eaten. Ashkenazic Jews, from Central and Eastern Europe, where there is less of a tradition of eating lamb, will more likely serve chicken, turkey, or fish at Passover.

Gefilte fish is a traditional Ashkenazic dish served at Passover, as well as on the

Sabbath and other festivals. *Gefilte* (pronounced ge-FILL-tah) means "stuffed." The fish's flesh was originally taken from the bones, minced, seasoned, and put back into its skin. The fish was then baked in the oven. Some cooks used the easier method of forming the flesh into balls or ovals and poaching them in fish stock. This is how it is nearly always done today. However, the older name lingers, although an actual stuffed fish is hardly ever seen.

Making gefilte fish is a time-consuming process. Many people now use the very good commercial brands that are available.

Jewish people are required to eat matzah during the Seder, but there is no obligation to eat it at any other time. Nevertheless, most do eat matzah during Passover since it is the only form of bread allowed. Some Ashkenazic rabbis go even further and ban grains that resemble the ones used for making bread. They prohibit food made from *kitniyot*, a category that includes beans, peas, and rice, as well as such grains as corn, millet, and buckwheat. A few are even more strict, banning garlic, mustard, sesame, and sunflower seeds, as well as sunflower and safflower oil.

Sephardic rabbis disagree. They permit these foods, largely because they form a large part of the Middle Eastern diet. People would have nothing to eat. Actual practice varies among Sephardic communities. Some eat beans, but not rice; others eat rice, but not beans. Some avoid garbanzo beans, also known as chickpeas, because their Hebrew name, *humus*, sounds like *chametz* (leavening).

Spring vegetables that are just coming into season, such as asparagus and fava beans, are also traditionally found on the Passover table. They symbolize new life being reborn after the dark winter of slavery.

Favorite Passover Recipes

HUEVOS HAMINADOS

The Passover meal begins by eating eggs. An egg is prominently displayed on the Seder plate. Eggs are a symbol of fertility, of life overcoming death. Eggs also symbolize the Jewish people, since eggs are the only food that grows harder the more they are cooked. So, too, have our hardships throughout the ages made us stronger.

Huevos haminados is a traditional Sephardic dish served on the Sabbath and on festivals, especially Passover.

Brown skins from 12 large onions
12 large raw eggs in their shells
4 quarts of water
3 tablespoons oil

Line the bottom of a large pot with the onion skins. Place the eggs on top and pour in enough water to cover them.

Bring the water to a boil. Add the oil, cover the pot, and allow the eggs to simmer over a very low flame for 8 to 12 hours. They will be a rich brown color, both inside and out.

Remove the eggshells. Serve warm or at room temperature.

Preparing food for the Seder. In this contemporary pop-up book, the figures' arms move when the red tab is pulled. (From The Haggada of Passover, *adapted from the medieval Bird's-head Haggada.)*

הכנת חרוסת
לקערת הסדר

**PREPARING
HAROSET FOR
THE SEDER**

CHAROSET

Charoset is the sweet mixture of fruit, nuts, and wine that symbolizes the mortar that held together the bricks used by the Israelites to build cities for Pharaoh.

Here are two equally tasty charoset recipes; one from Ashkenazic or European tradition, the other from the Sephardic or Middle Eastern tradition. While charoset is traditionally used as part of the Seder ritual, these delicious, sweet fruit mixtures can be served as one would serve a cranberry sauce with the meal.

ASHKENAZIC CHAROSET

3 large apples (about 1 pound),
   unpeeled, cored, and cut into large pieces
1 cup chopped almonds or walnuts
2 tablespoons honey
1 teaspoon ground cinnamon
1 cup sweet red wine or grape juice

Combine the apples, nuts, honey, and cinnamon in a food processor. Stir in enough wine or grape juice to make a paste that holds together. Store in the refrigerator. Serve at room temperature.

Another variation is to coarsely grate the apples and mix the other ingredients by hand, for a chunkier charoset.

SEPHARDIC CHAROSET

1⅓ cups chopped pitted dates
¾ to 1 cup chopped walnuts or almonds
About ¼ cup sweet red wine or grape juice

Combine the dates and nuts in a food processor, adding enough wine or grape juice to make a thick paste. The mixture will be sweet, but honey can be added to make it sweeter. Store in the refrigerator. Serve at room temperature.

TZIMMES

A tzimmes is a fruit and vegetable stew, and a very popular dish among Ashkenazic Jews. Because a tzimmes contains a number of different ingredients, preparing one requires several steps. Hence the expression, "Don't make a tzimmes," which means "Don't make a fuss."

3 carrots, peeled and sliced ½ cup brown sugar
4 sweet potatoes, peeled and sliced ⅛ teaspoon salt
3 tart apples ⅛ teaspoon white pepper
4 tablespoons oil 1 cup water

Cook the carrots and sweet potato slices in a saucepan until tender. Drain off excess liquid. Peel, quarter, and cut the apples into ¼-inch slices.

Oil a 2 ½ quart casserole. Cover the bottom with a layer of carrots, then a

layer of apples, then a layer of sweet potatoes. Season each layer with brown sugar, salt, pepper, and oil. Continue layering until all the ingredients are used. Add the water.

Cover the casserole. Bake in a preheated, 350 degrees Fahrenheit oven for 30 minutes, or until the apples are tender. Remove the cover and continue baking until the top is golden brown.

SWEET POTATO KUGEL

6 small raw sweet potatoes, peeled	2 teaspoons cinnamon
3 small raw apples, peeled	6 whole cloves
2 raw carrots, peeled	3 cardamom pods
1/4 cup brown sugar	1 cup chopped walnuts
1 cup dates, chopped	1/4 cup orange juice
1/4 cup matzoh meal	2 tablespoons olive oil

Preheat the oven to 375 degrees Fahrenheit.

Grate apples, sweet potatoes, and carrots in a food processor or by hand. Mix all the ingredients together in a large bowl. Pour into a 9″ x 9″ pan and bake for 45 minutes until the top is brown and crisp, and the middle is soft and well cooked.

POTATO KUGEL

Potatoes originated in South America. They did not appear in Europe until the sixteenth century. Sir Walter Raleigh first planted them on his estates in Ireland. From there they spread throughout Europe, becoming popular as a cheap food source. Most Jewish people in Eastern Europe lived on a diet of potatoes. Potato kugel is a potato pudding, a delicious popular dish frequently served on the Sabbath and for festivals.

6 potatoes	2 eggs, beaten well
1 carrot	1/4 cup salad oil
1 onion	1/2 teaspoon salt
1/4 cup matzah meal	Pepper to taste

Preheat the oven to 350 degrees Fahrenheit.

Put the potatoes, carrot, and onion through the coarsest grating blade of a food processor. Mix well with the remainder of the ingredients.

Bake uncovered in an oiled 9-inch x 9-inch pan for one hour. The top should be golden brown. Taste from the middle to make sure the potatoes are soft and very well done.

Hint: Make sure to cook the potato mixture right away to keep the kugel from turning gray or black. It should be snowy white to pink. Serve plain, or with gravy.

MRS. BERGER'S ALMOND MACAROONS

Making Passover desserts has always been a challenge since flour cannot be used. Macaroons have become a traditional dessert on Passover since they are made from a sweet, flourless paste. These are a lovely change from traditional coconut macaroons.

2 eggs, separated	1 teaspoon vanilla
2 cups ground almonds	Almond slivers or pieces of chopped
$\frac{1}{2}$ cup sugar	or broken almonds for decoration

Preheat the oven to 400 degrees Fahrenheit.

Mix the egg yolks, sugar, and vanilla to make a pale yellow mixture. Stir in the ground almonds with a spatula. Set aside.

Beat the egg whites lightly in a clean, dry bowl. Stop before peaks form. Fold the whites into the mixture.

Roll the mixture into small balls, flatten slightly, and place on a baking sheet lined with parchment paper. Put an almond sliver or almond piece on top of each macaroon.

Bake for 9 to 10 minutes, until the macaroons are lightly browned.

Allow to cool. Store in an airtight container. The macaroons will taste even better after a day or two.

Tzafun

DISTRIBUTE THE AFIKOMAN

The afikoman is the broken half of the middle matzah that the leader hid at the beginning of the Seder. In many families, it is the custom for children to find it and hide it away themselves. The leader must offer a reward to get the afikoman back. Other families give a prize to the child who finds the afikoman first.

The afikoman must always be the last bite eaten at the Seder meal. Without it, the meal cannot come to an end. The afikoman must be found because the Seder must conclude by midnight.

Hiding the afikoman is a European Passover tradition. It is not usually practiced in North Africa and the Middle East. The opportunity to hide the afikoman encourages children to pay attention and remain awake until the end of the Seder.

The word *afikoman* comes from a Greek word, although no one is certain which one. The most likely candidate is *epikomios*, which means a "festive procession." The ancient Greeks and Romans concluded a banquet by parading through the streets to visit their friends. This kept the party going all night.

The rabbis disapproved of such revelry on the holy night of Passover. That is why the Mishnah says that there must be no "afikoman" after the Passover meal. Over the years, the Greek word came to be applied to the dessert, then eventually to the last piece of the middle matzah, which concludes the meal. No other food can be eaten after the guests have finished the afikoman.

This is because the Passover meal must end with matzah. According to some rabbis, the last piece of matzah represents the Passover lamb, whose taste should linger in our mouths at the end of the meal. Since we no longer have a real Passover lamb, the matzah takes its place.

Other rabbis disagree. The Seder began with *Ha Lachma Anya*, the bread of poverty, which is matzah. As it began with matzah, so must it conclude with matzah. We should end the Seder with the taste of matzah in our mouths as a reminder that we are still "in Egypt." War, slavery, poverty, oppression, and injustice have not yet come to an end. Until they do, the whole world is "Egypt" and we are still slaves in exile.

There is another, more hopeful, view of the

afikoman. Only after we have eaten the last of the matzah, the "bread of poverty," do we truly become free people.

People once believed the afikoman had magical powers. They would save afikoman crumbs as charms to bring good luck or ward off evil spirits. A woman giving birth might be given a piece of afikoman to clutch in her hand to protect her and her baby.

A seven-year-old piece of afikoman supposedly had the power to stop floods if thrown into the rising waters. Tossing a piece of afikoman into the ocean during a storm would calm the sea and ensure a safe journey. During the Middle Ages, Jewish merchants and sailors hid pieces of afikoman aboard their ships to prevent them from sinking.

According to one belief, a bit of afikoman placed in a bin of rice or flour made sure the bin never became empty during the coming year.

TZEDAKAH

Many children do not ransom the afikoman for themselves. They donate the gifts or money they receive to charity projects that help others. Mazon is one such project. *Mazon* is the Hebrew word for "food." Money donated by Jewish people in America is used to purchase and distribute food to needy people. Nothing could be more in keeping with the spirit of Passover than to donate the afikoman ransom to Mazon.

If you or your family would like to contribute to Mazon, or learn more about it, write to this address:

MAZON: A JEWISH RESPONSE TO HUNGER
1990 South Bundy Drive/Suite 260
Los Angeles, CA 90025-5232

You may also visit Mazon's Web site at www.mazon.org.

The Passover meal is over. We're coming to the end of the Seder. First, we need the afikoman. Where is it? Do you know?

I Am the Afikoman

LYRICS BY DEBBIE FRIEDMAN

I'm over here, come find me. I'm hiding in the books.

I see you getting closer, but I can't get you to look.

You do not seem to see me, but I am looking right at you.

I am the afikoman, and hiding's what I do.

Someone takes the middle matzah, and they break it into two.

I become one half of it; then I am hidden far from you.

They wrap me in a napkin, so I don't get crumbs around.

Then someone buys me back after I've been found.

I'm over here. I'm hiding. You'll find me if you try.

I see you getting closer, but then you walk right by.

You do not seem to see me but I'm looking right at you.

I am the afikoman, and hiding's what I do.

Barech

GRACE AFTER MEALS

The Passover meal comes to an end after the guests have eaten the afikoman. Together we recite the *Birkat Hamazon*, a long series of blessings thanking God for the food we have eaten. It begins with these words:

Praised are You, God, Ruler of Creation, who sustains the entire world with goodness, kindness, and mercy. God gives food to all creatures, for God's mercy lasts forever. Because of God's abundant goodness, we have never known want. May we never be in need, for the sake of God's name. God is the one who nourishes, sustains, and provides for all living creatures.

The *Birkat Hamazon* is an ancient prayer that has grown over the centuries as more and more blessings have been added. Its roots go back to the earliest days of the Jewish people.

Tradition says that the first part of the prayer was recited by Moses to thank God for the gift of manna, the miraculous food that fed the Children of Israel during the forty years they wandered in the desert.

The second part offers thanks for the Land of Israel, which God gave to our ancestors as an inheritance. This part was recited by Joshua as he led the Twelve Tribes of Israel across the Jordan River into the land of Canaan.

The third part was recited by King Solomon upon completion of the building of the Temple in Jerusalem.

Elijah's Cup

Grace after meals is completed. The Seder guests recite the blessing over wine and drink the third cup. The cups are refilled a fourth time. Then the leader goes to the door and opens it wide. Everyone at the Seder looks toward the doorway, and then watches Elijah's Cup of wine, standing in the center of the table. Does some of the wine disappear? Has Elijah come to our house?

Elijah was one of the greatest prophets in the Bible. He lived in the kingdom of Israel during the ninth century B.C.E. The Second Book of Kings (Kings II 2:1–12) tells how he was taken up to heaven in a chariot of fire. Because Elijah never died, it is said that he still lives. According to countless legends, he returns to earth in disguise to help people in need. At the end of time Elijah will come again, bringing with him the Messiah, the anointed king, who will rule forever in peace and justice.

Together we sing the following song, in honor of Elijah.

Eliyahu, ha-Navi

Eliyahu, haNavi.	Elijah, the Prophet.
Eliyahu, haTishbi.	Elijah, the Tishbite.
Eliyahu, Eliyahu,	Elijah, Elijah,
Eliyahu, haGiladi.	Elijah, of Gilead.
Bimhayrah b'yamenu	Soon, during our lifetime
Yavo eleynu	He will come to us
Im Mashiach ben David,	With the Messiah, the son of David,
Im Mashiach ben David.	With the Messiah, the son of David.

Passover Feast in Russia, 1949. Elijah, always a welcome guest in every home, is greeted with awe and surprise — or is it suspicion — in this depiction of a Seder in post-war Russia. (Max Berger. Vienna, Austria.)

שבט

חֲמָתְךָ אֶל הַגּוֹיִם
אֲשֶׁר לֹא יְדָעוּךָ וְעַל
הַמַּמְלָכוֹת אֲשֶׁר
בְּשִׁמְךָ לֹא
קָרָאוּ

שְׁפוֹךְ עֲלֵיהֶם זַעְמֶךָ וַחֲרוֹן
אַפְּךָ יַשִּׂיגֵם תִּרְדֹּף בְּאַף
וְתַשְׁמִירֵם מִתַּחַת שְׁמֵי יְיָ

Elijah the Builder

RETOLD BY PENINNAH SCHRAM

This story about Elijah comes from the Talmud. It dates back to Israel in the third century C.E.
It is one of the earliest tales of how Elijah returns to help someone in need.

There was once a good, pious couple who had five children. But rich as they were in faith and family, so poor were they in wealth. Now the husband had not been able to find work for many weeks.

One day, when they did not have enough bread to put on the table, and the children cried from hunger, the wife said, "Husband, go to the marketplace. Maybe today God on High will help you find some work so you can earn a few pennies. We must not give up hope. God will help you, but not if you just sit at home."

And her husband answered, "Where can I go that I haven't been? What new doors can I knock on that I haven't tried? I have no rich relatives, no rich friends — not that I would bring shame on us by borrowing from anyone."

However, each day the situation became worse, and finally the wife cried, "How can you sit and watch your children die before your eyes? Go, husband, trust in God. May God bring you hope so you may prosper."

Reluctantly, the husband left the house, walked a little way in one direction, then in another, and finally he sank to the ground, looked up at the heavens, and prayed: "Great God in the heavens, great and good God. Take pity on us; have mercy on my little children. For their sake, if not for mine, help us. Our hunger is terrible and we ask, we plead with You, O Merciful God, You who created us, hear my prayers and turn to us in Your mercy and send Your help — or else let me die now and quickly, so I should no longer see how my children and my wife suffer."

And then he rose and walked on as in a daze, weeping and praying. Suddenly, a young man appeared on the road walking toward the unfortunate husband. He stopped and asked the unhappy man what troubled him so. And the unfortunate husband began to weep again, as he told his story of misery. Then the young man, who was Elijah the Prophet in disguise, said, "Take me to the marketplace and sell me to the person I will point out to you. When you receive the agreed-upon price, give me one dinar. That is all you have to do."

"Good sir," said the astonished husband, "you are kind in offering to help, but you look more like

The Messiah Enters Jerusalem. *This piece depicts a traditional image of the prophet Elijah heralding the arrival of the Messiah. (1560 Mantuan adaptation of one of the pages in the Prague Haggadah of 1526.)*

my master and I your slave. They will never believe me when I look like this." And the man pointed to his rags and bare feet.

But Elijah insisted, "Do as I tell you, and all will be well with you. Come, and we'll go to the auction."

As they walked through the marketplace, many did mistake the man for Elijah's slave, but Elijah told them, "No, he is my master."

It happened that one of the king's ministers had come riding through to buy slaves for the building of the king's new palace. Upon seeing the strong young man, the minister began to bid for him as soon as Elijah was called up for sale. When the king's minister offered the price of eighty dinars, Elijah said quickly to the man, "Sell me to the one who bid eighty dinars, and do not accept any more bids." The man took the eighty dinars and gave one dinar to Elijah as he had promised. Elijah held the dinar in his hand for a moment and then said, "Take this dinar now and return home. May it be for good. You will never suffer from poverty or want again." And he blessed the man.

When Elijah rode off with the king's minister, the man bought all kinds of good food and returned home.

After his family had eaten, the wife said, "My husband, you did what I advised, and it seems as if I gave you good counsel. But tell me how this came to pass. How did you earn this money?" And her husband told her how he had met the young man and sold him as a slave. He often wondered what happened to that young man and who he really was.

When Elijah left with the king's minister, he was brought to the king. The king had been planning to build a great palace outside the city and had bought many slaves to haul stones, timber, and other building materials. As soon as the king saw Elijah he asked, "And do you have a particular skill or shall we put you to work with all the slaves to drag stones and cut trees?"

"I am a builder, your Majesty," said Elijah, "and I can work best by planning and directing the work."

"Well, then, it is our good fortune that we have purchased you today," said the king, and he explained his plan for the great palace he desired to

have built. "Build it for me in six months' time, and I will reward you greatly and also grant you your freedom."

"Your Majesty," replied Elijah, "I will do as you ask in even a shorter time. Have the slaves prepare all the building materials at once."

The king directed all the slaves to do as Elijah had asked.

That night, Elijah prayed that God Most High perform a miracle and build the palace according to the king's wishes.

And a miracle happened. All the angels came down from the heavens and worked together to build a magnificent palace. As soon as it was dawn, the palace was finished and Elijah knew the king would be pleased. And when Elijah saw that the angels had finished their work and returned to the heavens, he, too, disappeared.

In the morning, the slaves arose for the day's work, but, to their astonishment, they saw the completed palace. They ran to the king, who then searched for his chief builder.

"He must have been one of the angels," the king said when he could not find Elijah anywhere.

"But," he added with a grand gesture as though speaking to the air, "I release you and declare you a free man."

One day Elijah met the man who had sold him, and the man asked him, "Tell me, how did you fare when you were brought to the king?"

And Elijah answered, "I could have freed myself immediately; but a promise is a promise, and he had paid good money for me to work. So I built him a great palace as he asked. I did not want him to regret buying me and paying so much gold. I performed a task for him worth many times over what he had paid for me. After I fulfilled my promise, I left."

Then the man understood that this was Elijah and thanked him many times and said, "You have restored me to life."

As time passed, the couple acquired even greater good fortune; and they were blessed for the rest of their lives, grateful to God Most High for all that they now had in their lives.

Miriam's Cup

Many people follow a new tradition at their Seders. A cup of water is placed beside Elijah's Cup. This is Miriam's Cup. It honors the Prophet Miriam, Moses' sister, who played an important part in the Passover story. Were it not for Miriam, Moses would never have been born.

A midrash, or legend, explains that Miriam's father, Amram, wanted to divorce his wife, Jochebed. He no longer wished to be married. Why bring children into the world who would only grow up to become slaves? Better for them never to be born.

Miriam rebuked her father with these words:

"Father, you are more cruel than Pharaoh. Pharaoh wants to get rid of the boy babies. You would get rid of the girl babies, too. Pharaoh deprives his victims of life in this world. If you prevent children from being born, you deprive them not only of life in this world, but of eternal life in the world to come.

"I believe that God will not abandon us. God is mightier than Pharaoh. God will fulfill the promise to bring us out of Egypt. But we must do our part. We must continue to believe in God. If we lose hope and cease to have children, we will no longer exist as a people. In a few generations we will disappear.

These are three Miriam's Cups by contemporary American artists. The first piece (immediate right), The Dance with Timbrels *by Kathy Hart, is made of sterling silver and garnet. The chains and beads make music when they are moved, and woven textures remind us of Moses' basket.* Miriam's Glass *(middle), by Carol Hamoy, is made from* yahrzeit *glasses, bells, and shells. The* yahrzeit *glasses commemorate those persons, including the Egyptians, who were unable to cross the Red Sea. It is a reminder of God's compassion for all people. Also, the glass makes comforting, sweet music when moved.* Miriam's Dance *(far right), by Susan Fischerweis, is made from polymer clay (and miscellaneous findings). Water is the underlying theme. As Miriam joyously dances, the waters pour forth from the well. The waters gather symbolically into a wave of the parted Red Sea. Many people now create their own unique Miriam's Cups using personal items that are both sentimental and symbolic.*

This is what Pharaoh wants. Don't you see, Father? You yourself would give Pharaoh the victory that God would deny him."

Miriam's words convinced Amram. He returned to his wife. Within a year Moses was born.

Miriam's Cup is filled with water because water is important to her story. Miriam watched over her brother Moses when he was set adrift in the Nile River. The magical fountain that followed the Israelites through the desert was called Miriam's Well. At the Red Sea, it was Miriam who led the Children of Israel between the waters. She and the women of Israel danced and sang to celebrate the victory over Pharaoh.

This is the song that Miriam sang on the shores of the Red Sea. It appears in Exodus 15:1-11.

I will sing to You, God, for You are great.
Horse and rider You hurled into the sea.
Your strength was my salvation. You are my God. I will exalt You.
You are master of war. Almighty God is Your name.
You threw Pharaoh's army into the ocean.
The captains of Your legions sank into the quicksand.
Deep water covered them. They sank like stones to the bottom. . . .
Who is like You, God, among the heavens? Who is like You, wrapped in Holiness,
Frightening in majesty, working miracles?

Miriam's Song

LYRICS BY DEBBIE FRIEDMAN
BASED ON EXODUS 15:2-21

Whenever this song is sung, all the women rise up and dance!

CHORUS
And the women dancing with their timbrels
Followed Miriam as she sang her song.
Sing a song to the One whom we've exalted.
Miriam and the women danced and danced the whole night long.

And Miriam was a weaver of unique variety.
The tapestry she wove was one which sang our history.
With every strand and every thread she crafted her delight.
A woman touched with spirit, she dances toward the light.

CHORUS

When Miriam stood upon the shores and gazed across the sea,
The wonder of this miracle she soon came to believe.
Whoever thought the sea would part with an outstretched hand,
And we would pass to freedom, and march to the promised land.

CHORUS

And Miriam the Prophet took her timbrel in her hand,
And all the women followed her just as she had planned.
And Miriam raised her voice in song.
She sang with praise and might.
We've just lived through a miracle; we're going to dance tonight.

CHORUS

Detail from The Song of Miriam the Prophetess.
(William Gale, nineteenth-century British artist.)

Hallel

SING SONGS OF PRAISE AND FREEDOM

The door is closed. The leader returns to the table and leads the guests in singing the Hallel.

Praise God, all you nations! Praise God, all you peoples! God's kindness overwhelms us. God's truth lasts forever. Hallelujah!

Psalm 117 is one of several Psalms included in the Hallel. The word *hallel* means "praise." It is the first part of the word *hallelujah*, which came into English from Hebrew. Hallelujah means "praise God."

The Hallel consists of hymns from the Book of Psalms that were sung by choirs of Levites in the Temple. It was sung on the great festivals, when throngs of pilgrims packed Jerusalem's streets. On Passover the Levites sang the Hallel twice: once in the afternoon while the lambs were being sacrificed, and again in the evening when families and friends came together to share the Passover meal.

The Psalms and stories of the Bible, especially the Passover story of the going-forth from Egypt, inspired brilliant music in another tradition — that of African-Americans, whose ancestors were held in bondage as long and bitter as that of the Israelites in Egypt.

Like the Israelites, the slaves did not despair. They knew that God had not abandoned them. They believed that the day of deliverance was coming, when, as the Bible promised, God would break their chains and split the waters, leading them forth from Egypt into the promised land.

Let us join our voices with theirs.

Go Down, Moses

This famous African-American spiritual is sung at many Seders. Harriet Tubman, who guided runaway slaves along the Underground Railroad, was known as Moses.

When Israel was in Egypt's land,
    Let my people go.
Oppressed so hard they could not stand,
    Let my people go.

CHORUS:
Go down, Moses,
Way down in Egypt's land.
Tell old Pharaoh
To let my people go.

"Thus saith the Lord," bold Moses said.
    Let my people go.
"If not, I'll strike your firstborn dead."
    Let my people go.

CHORUS

No more shall they in bondage toil.
    Let my people go.
Let them come out with Egypt's spoil.
    Let my people go.

CHORUS

We need not always weep and mourn.
    Let my people go.
And wear these slavery chains forlorn.
    Let my people go.

CHORUS

Your foes shall not forever stand.
    Let my people go.
You shall possess your own good land.
    Let my people go.

CHORUS

Oh let us all from bondage flee.
    Let my people go.
And soon may all the earth be free.
    Let my people go.

CHORUS

For generations, the African men, women, and children held in bondage in America longed to be free.
(Jerry Pinkney, from the "Let My People Go" section of From Sea to Shining Sea. *New York, 1993.)*

Nishmat Kol Chai

THE SOUL OF EVERY LIVING BEING

The Hallel is followed by a very old and beautiful prayer called the Nishmat Kol Chai, which means "The Soul of Every Living Being." Its oldest part goes back to the first century C.E. to the time of the Temple. A curious legend circulated during the Middle Ages that this prayer was originally composed by Saint Peter. Although this idea has been rejected by Jewish commentators, it is not too hard to imagine members of the earliest Christian community composing a beautiful prayer that found its way into the larger Jewish population. The earliest Christians, after all, were Jews who lived in Jerusalem. If so, it is a gift that ought to be treasured, for the Nishmat is one of the most moving of all Jewish prayers.

If our mouths were filled with song as the sea,

And our tongues with praise like the rolling waves;

If our lips were as full of devotion as the sky above,

And our eyes shining forth like the sun and the moon;

If we stretched out our hands in prayer like the wings of soaring eagles,

And if our feet possessed the swiftness of gazelles —

We would still be unable to thank you and praise you enough,

Our God and God of our ancestors,

For the smallest portion of the countless

Hundreds,

Thousands,

Millions of blessings

You have given our ancestors and ourselves.

Nirtzah

THE END OF THE SEDER

We say the blessings and drink the last of the four cups of wine.

בָּרוּךְ אַתָּה יְיָ אֱלֹהֵינוּ מֶלֶךְ הָעוֹלָם בּוֹרֵא פְּרִי הַגָּפֶן.

Baruch ata Adonai, Eloheinu Melech ha-olam borei p'ri ha-gafen.

Praised are You, God, Ruler of Creation, who created the fruit of the vine.

Another blessing follows, expressing the hope that we may soon return to the land of Israel, to walk through the streets of a restored Jerusalem and offer our sacrifices at a new Temple. We thank God for the land and the fruit of the vine.

Nirtzah, the final portion of the Haggadah, now begins. Our journey is near its end. The exact meaning of Nirtzah is unclear. It probably means "acceptance." We hope that God will find our Seder acceptable, for we have done our best to fulfill the spirit, as well as the rules and details of the Passover meal.

We express this hope by reciting verses from a poem written a thousand years ago by Rabbi Joseph Bonfils, who lived in France at the time of the First Crusade.

Jews returning to Jerusalem. The Temple on top resembles a medieval cathedral.
(Birds Head Haggadah. Southern Germany, c. 1300.)

The complete poem summarizes all the laws of Passover in rhyme. The poem was read in synagogues on the Sabbath before Passover. The verse below represents the last part of Rabbi Bonfils' poem:

Our Seder now at last is done.

God's laws we've followed, every one.

May our friends who've gathered here

Join again with us next year.

God, look down from heaven above.

Bless us all with peace and love.

Bring us to Zion, in our days,

Where we will shout with songs of praise:

לְשָׁנָה הַבָּאָה בִּירוּשָׁלָיִם!

L'shanah Haba-ah birushalayim!

Next year in Jerusalem!

Echad Mi Yodeah?

Several rousing songs bring the Seder to its close. "Echad Mi Yodeah?" "Who Knows One?" is a cumulative counting song for children that first appeared in a sixteenth-century German Haggadah. Its verses go from one to thirteen, beginning and ending with God. The first verse affirms the oneness of God, which is the core belief of the Jewish religion.

Echad mi yodeah? Echad ani yodeah.

Echad eloheinu shebashamayim uvaaretz.

Who knows One? I know One!

One is our God who rules heaven and earth.

Shnayim mi yodeah? Shnayim ani yodeah.

Shnei luchot habrit,

Echad eloheinu shebashamayim uvaaretz.

Etc. . . .

Who knows Two? I know Two!

Two are the tablets of God's Law.

One is our God who rules heaven and earth.

Etc. . . .

Sh'losha avot.

Arba imahot.

Chamishah chumshei Torah.

Shishah sidrei Mishnah.

Shivah y'mei shabatah.

Sh'monah y'mei milah.

Tishah yarchei leidah.

Asarah dibraya.

Echad asar kochvaya.

Sh'neim asar shivtaya.

Sh'loshah asar midaya.

Three are the patriarchs.

Four are the matriarchs.

Five are the books of the Torah.

Six are the volumes of the Mishnah.

Seven is the Sabbath day.

Eight are the days before Milah.

Nine are the months to bear a child.

Ten are the Ten Commandments.

Eleven are the stars in Joseph's dream.

Twelve are Israel's tribes.

Thirteen are the attributes of God.

Chad Gadya

"Chad Gadya" or "One Little Goat," is the best known of the traditional songs included in the Haggadah. It tells the cumulative story of a little goat "that Father bought for two *zuzim*." A *zuz* is a small coin, like a penny. A cat eats the goat, a dog eats the cat, a stick beats the dog, and so on, as the stronger creatures devour the weaker ones. But in the last verse, "The Holy One," overcomes Death.

1. Chad gadya, chad gadya.
   Dizvan abba bitrei zuzei.
   Chad gadya, chad gadya.

   One little goat, one little goat.
   That Father bought for two zuzim.
   One little goat, one little goat.

2. V'ata shunra v'achal l'gadya.
   Dizvan abba bitrei zuzei.
   Chad gadya, chad gadya.

   There came a cat who ate the goat.
   That Father bought for two zuzim.
   One little goat, one little goat.

3. V'ata chalba v'nashach l'shunra . . .

   There came a dog that bit the cat . . .

4. V'ata chutra v'hikah l'chalba . . .

   There came a stick that beat the dog . . .

5. V'ata nurah v'saraf l'chutra . . .

   There came a fire that burnt the stick . . .

6. V'ata maya v'chava l'nurah . . .

   The water came that quenched the fire . . .

7. V'ata torah v'shata l'maya . . .

The ox came and drank the water . . .

8. V'ata shochet v'shachat l'tora . . .

Then came the butcher who killed the ox . . .

9. V'ata malach hamavet v'shachat l'shochet . . .

And the Angel of Death came and killed the butcher . . .

10. V'ata Ha-Kadosh Baruch v'shachat l'malach . . .

And then came the Holy One who killed the Angel of Death . . .

Hatikvah

"Hatikvah" (The Hope) was composed by Naftali Herz Imber in 1878 to commemorate the founding of the first Jewish settlement in Israel. Since then it has become the anthem of the State of Israel and of Jewish people throughout the world.

Kol od balevav p'nimah	Deep within the darkest hours of night,
Nefesh Y'hudi homiyah	Jewish souls are yearning for the light.
Ulfaatei mizrach kadimah	Turning to the east to greet the dawn
Ayin l'Tzion tzofiyah.	Facing Zion, where our hope is born.
Od lo avdah tikvatenu	Our hope, through all the bitter years.
Hatikvah bat sh'not alpayim:	Our hope, through all our trials and tears,
Lih'yot am chofshi b'artzenu	To return, a free people once again,
B'Eretz Tzion, Vi'rushalayim.	To Israel, Zion, and Jerusalem.

The Temple in Jerusalem from the Leipnik Haggadah.
(Darmstadt, 1733.)

BIBLIOGRAPHY

Many sources were used in preparing this book. The following are the ones I found to be the most valuable.

Ben-Sasson, H. H., ed. *A History of the Jewish People*. Cambridge: Harvard University Press, 1976.

Birnbaum, Philip. Translated and annotated by the author. *The Passover Haggadah*. New York: Hebrew Publishing Company, 1953.

Elias, Rabbi Joseph. *The Haggadah: With Translation and a New Commentary Based on Talmudic, Midrashic, and Rabbinic Sources*. Brooklyn, New York: Mesorah Publications, 1995.

Encyclopedia Judaica (vol. 13). New York: Macmillan, 1971. "Passover"

Ginzburg, Louis. *Legends of the Jews (vols. II & III)*. Philadelphia: The Jewish Publication Society of America, 1969.

Glenn, M. G. Selected and translated by the author. *Jewish Tales and Legends*. New York: Hebrew Publishing Company, 1929.

Goodman, Philip, ed. *The Passover Anthology*. Philadelphia: The Jewish Publication Society of America, 1971.

Jaffe, Nina. Illustrated by Elivier Savadier. *The Mysterious Visitor: Stories of the Prophet Elijah*. New York: Scholastic Press, 1997.

Levi, Shonie B., and Sylvia R. Kaplan. *Guide for the Jewish Homemaker*. New York: Schocken Books, 1972.

Millgram, Abraham. *Jewish Worship*. Philadelphia: The Jewish Publication Society of America, 1971.

Musleah, Rahel. Illustrated by Louise August. *Why On This Night? A Passover Haggadah for Family Celebration*. New York: Simon & Schuster, 2000.

Raphael, Chaim. *A Feast of History: The Drama of Passover Through the Ages*. Washington, D.C.: B'nai Brith Books, 1993.

Vilnay, Zev. *Legends of Jerusalem*. Philadelphia: The Jewish Publication Society of America, 1973.

Wallach, Rabbi Shalom Meir. *Haggadah of the Chassidic Masters*. Brooklyn, New York: Mesorah Publications, 1990.

Yerushalmi, Yosef Hayim. *Haggadah and History: A Panorama in Facsimile of Five Centuries of the Printed Haggadah*. Philadelphia: Jewish Publication Society of America, 1975.

CREDITS

Pages: viii: British Library, London; 2: British Library, London/Bridgeman Art Library, New York; 4: SuperStock, Jacksonville, Florida; 6 (and pages 13, 18, 19, 20, 33, 94, 95, 96, 97, 98, 106, 109, 120, and 125): used by permission from Yedioth Abronoth Books, Tel Aviv, Israel; 10: David Harris, Jerusalem; 12: Granger Collection, New York; 14: courtesy of Feldheim Publishers, Nanuet, New York; 16: permission granted by the Estate of Arthur Szyk; 21: Art Resource, New York; 22: Granger Collection; 24: illustration by Anita Lobel in *From Sea to Shining Sea* by Amy L. Cohn. Illustration copyright © 1993 by Anita Lobel. Used by permission; 27: Jewish Museum, New York/Art Resource; 28: Granger Collection; 30: Israel Museum, Jerusalem/Kid's Books, Chicago; 32: Wolfson Museum in Hechal Shlomo, Jerusalem; 37: Granger Collection; 39: collection of the editor; 40: Mary Evans Picture Library, London; 44: reprinted from *The Best of K'tonton*, copyright © 1980 by The Jewish Publication Society, Philadelphia, Pennsylvania; 46: British Library/Bridgeman Art Library; 50: permission granted by the Estate of Arthur Szyk; 57 and 59: Heritage-Images, London/copyright © The British Library; 63: Eric Lessing/Art Resource; 66: Mary Evans Picture Library; 70–71: *Exodus*, oil painting by David Sharir, courtesy of Pucker Gallery, Inc., Boston, Massachusetts; 73: painting by Michal Meron, courtesy of thestudioinoldjaffa.com; 75: Granger Collection; 76 (and pages 77, 78, and 79): courtesy of Feldheim Publishers; 82: David Harris/Israel Museum, Jerusalem; 84: courtesy of The Long Island Committee for Soviet Jewry, New York; 87: courtesy of The Jewish Theological Seminary of America, New York; 92: Darmstadt Technical University, Germany; 101: Israel Museum, Jerusalem/Kid's Books, Chicago, Illinois; 110: Art Resource; 112: The Jewish Theological Seminary; 116: Kathy Hart, Southborough, Massachusetts; 117 (left): Carol Hamoy, New York, New York; 117 (right) Susan Fischer Weis, Northfield, New Jersey, all from the *Miriam's Cups* exhibit by Ma'yan: The Jewish Women's Project, New York, New York, 1997; 118: SuperStock; 122: illustration copyright © 1993 by Jerry Pinkney from the "Let My People Go" section of *From Sea to Shining Sea*, used by permission; 124: Israel Museum, Jerusalem; 131: Suzanne Kaufman/The Jewish Theological Seminary.

INDEX